A Step Up

By Pat Nolan

A Step Up

By Pat Nolan

First published 2013

Clachan Publishing

3 Drumavoley Park

Ballycastle

Glens of Antrim

BT54 6PE

ISBN : 978-1-909906-17-4

A Step Up

The arrival of BIM 56-footers further enhanced the part played in Irish fishing by their predecessors, the ground-breaking BIM 50-footers.

Pat Nolan

This book is dedicated to the men who built, owned, skippered and fished on BIM 56-footers.

Contents

Preface

In 2006 I set about tracing the histories of all eighty-eight BIM 50ft fishing boats built between 1949 and 1970 inclusive. Researching the topic was a labour of love that led to much travel and meeting up with many wonderful people. I sat and chatted for hours on end with men who fished on those iconic vessels of another era. Two years later the fruits of my endeavours came to fulfilment with the publication of *Sea Change*, a book based on the rise of the BIM 50-footer and its immense impact on coastal Ireland of the 1950s and '60s. On numerous occasions I have since been approached to carry out similar research on fishing vessels widely known as the BIM 56-footers. Those boats are regarded as a step up from the 50-footer. For awhile I resisted, but the 'bug' that is in me where those superb boats are concerned ensured that sooner or later I would capitulate and attempt the undertaking.

The book that has emerged contains details on each boat, and recollections of individuals who owned and/or fished on them.

This compilation is presented in two parts. Part I is based on comments, observations, experiences and memories relevant to the 56-footers. Part II is made up of individually traced histories of all thirty-nine BIM 56-footers built.

On my travels in search of information on the BIM 56-footers I occasionally met up with people who had unrelated, but nevertheless, interesting lifetime maritime experiences to recount. As such I have dedicated Part III of the book to the recollections, experiences and opinions of those people.

Acknowledgements

The recording of remarks, memories, experiences and anecdotes supplied by those who over the years were one way or another involved with BIM 56-footers, is my attempt at preserving the memory of the boats and the people associated with them. It may well be the one and only!! Time is marching on and none of us are getting any younger. Many thanks to those who so kindly responded to my pleas for information! Its information that occasionally came from unexpected quarters! For example I was surprised to receive a lengthy letter from John Niven with an address in the Strabane area of Co Tyrone. Strabane! Not a place one would immediately associate with BIM 56-footers. However there it was, a letter filled with snippets of information on the men and 56-footers that fished out of Burtonport in the early 1970s. It transpired that John, a close relative of the very well known Browne fishing family of Inch Island, Co Donegal, had considerable sea going experience and actually fished out of Burtonport during those early 1970s years. The information helped immensely with tying in boat ownership etc, much of which is included in Part 11 of the book.

Greatly appreciated too was the response from Billy Bates, Kilmore Quay, Co Wexford who sat down and wrote me a hand written letter furnishing information on five BIM 56-footers – the *Glendalough*, owned by his father, Willie Bates; the *Glenmalure*, owned by his uncle Jimmy Bates; the *Santa Lucia*, skippered by his uncle Mark Bates; the *Ard Ailbe*, a boat that fished out of Kilmore Quay and ended her days broken up on the slipway, and the *Guiding Star* a boat that also fished out of Kilmore Quay before being sold on.

As with my previous books, *Sea Change* and *Following the Shoals*, once again, without the immense co-operation and enthusiasm of *Marine Times Newspaper* Editor, Mark Mc Carthy, the gathering of material for this book would not have been possible. A special thanks to the ever so obliging Mark!

To all those persons, including my wife and family, who helped in any way to bring the book to fruition, I offer my most sincere thanks. A special thanks to my daughter, Carrie!

Introduction

In the introduction to my previous book, *Sea Change*, I mentioned that there was uncertainty as whether the Irish Sea Fisheries Association (ISFA) scheme under which 50ft boats were built and issued in the late 1940s resulted from fishermen pressure or the brainchild of ISFA personnel. Probably a bit of both! I further mentioned that regardless of whom or what prompted the scheme, it required the approval and support of the ISFA. I believe the initiation of the scheme has to go on record as one of immense importance to the Irish fishing industry and a venture for which credit has to be given to the ISFA, as indeed it does to An Bord Iascaigh Mhara (BIM), the body which continued to foster the scheme following the dissolution of the ISFA in 1952.

In the early 1950s when BIM 50-footers were beginning to pioneer a way forward for Irish fishermen, momentum was already gathering in some quarters for even bigger boats. When An Bord Iascaigh Mhara published its Third Annual Report (for year ended 31st March 1955) only three boats over 55ft were subject to hire purchase transactions. Those boats were not the 56-footers. However, the following passage did appear in the Report:

"During the year, following on notification from the Minister of Agriculture that a grant of £80,000 for the provision of fishing boats in the Fior-Gaeltacht* (Fior-Gaeltacht Boat Scheme**) had been approved, the Bord developed a vessel designed especially for this service, and arrangements are under way for the construction of a number of such vessels."

The passage was vague as to exactly what type or size of boat was planned for the *Fior-Gaeltacht*. A passage of similar length in the BIM Annual Report for year ending 31st March, 1956 provided further enlightenment. It read as follows:

"In accordance with the scheme for the provision of fishing boats in the Fior-Gaeltacht as announced by the Minister of Agriculture in the year 1954/55 the Board laid down at their own yards *** two vessels each 56'6" in length overall and equipped with 114h.p. diesel engines. By 31st March, 1956, one of these vessels had almost reached completion and substantial progress had been made on the second. An order had been placed with a boatyard other than those operated by the Board****for two vessels of similar design."

The specially designed vessel earlier referred to, later became known as the BIM 56-footer, though the actual overall length of boats built at BIM yards was 56'6". However, those built for BIM at Tyrrells Boatyard, were in fact exactly 56ft overall.

A Step Up

The BIM Annual Report for the year ending 31st March, 1957 updated its readers on the progress of the Fior-Gaeltacht Boat Scheme through the following extract,

"In May 1956 at Killybegs, Co Donegal, following the blessing by His Lordship, the Bishop of Raphoe, the Minister of Agriculture, Mr James Dillon, formally commissioned the first boat completed for the scheme. The vessel, Ard Macha, went into service under the command of Lieut. Patrick Gower, seconded from the Naval Service to train skipper designate P. MacFhionnlaigh (Joe McGinley)of Gola Island. On completion of the training course in December, 1956 skipper MacFhionnlaigh was placed in charge of the vessel which had been fishing satisfactorily since.

The second boat issued under the scheme, Ard Rathain, went into service in January, 1957 under the command of P. MacDonncdadha of Ceathramha Ruadha (Paric McDonagh, Carroe, Co Galway) and has been fishing successfully.

The third boat, Ard Mor, which was built at a private boatyard, was delivered to the Bord in March 1957 and arrangements were made to use it temporarily for training purposes of prospective skippers. At the close of the year a fourth boat was nearing completion at the private yard which had delivered the Ard Mor, and the keel of a fifth vessel was laid down during the year at one of the Bord's yards"

The above passage signalled the arrival of thirty-nine *similar* boats. While the *Ard Macha*, built at Killybegs, was numero uno, last built was the *Favourite*, launched at Dingle BIM Boatyard in December 1971. The boats would collectively be known as 'BIM 56-footers', and frequently referred to as '*Ard'* boats for obvious reasons.

*Foir-Gaeltacht is an expression used to describe areas of the country where the predominant language spoken is Irish. The exact definition has been a topic for discussion over the years.

** Under the auspices of the Fior-Gaeltacht Boat Scheme a deposit was not necessary from those to whom the boats were commissioned – *Seanad Eireann – Volume 46 – 18 July, 1956.*

*** Killybegs, Co Donegal (*Ard Macha*) and Mevagh, Co Donegal - (*Ard Rathain*).

**** Crosshaven Boatyard, Co Cork - (*Ard Mor* and *Ard Casta*).

The esteem in which the Minister of Agriculture of the day, Mr James Dillon, held the boats can be gleaned from a question and answer session on the crewing of the *Ard Macha* (Dail Eireann 07/June/1956 Ceisteanna). Mr Joseph Brennan, Fianna Fail T.D. for West Donegal put the questions:

Mr Brennan – Would the Minister not agree that it is both important and desirable to have the crew recruited from among the men of Teelin Gaeltacht who know the waters of the area so very well?

Mr. Dillon – I hope the boat will operate in much wider waters than those surrounding Teelin. If the boat is going to cruise up and down Teelin harbour I will be very disappointed. This is a 56 feet boat, the largest ever issued by Bord Iascaigh Mhara.

Mr Brennan – Will the Minister not agree that it must go in and out of Teelin harbour each day?

Mr Dillon – I hope to see it at sea for several days. The Deputy is getting out of date. This boat will be at sea for several days at a time. The Deputy will be dazzled when he sees this boat. When he sees three or four such boats along the coast he will get a weakness.

Following the *Ard Macha*, four further 56-footers were commissioned under the Fio-Gaeltacht Scheme; the *Ard Rathain* went into service in January, 1957 under the command of P. MacDonnchadha of Ceathramha Ruadha, Co Galway, the *Ard Mor* was delivered to the Bord in March 1957, and arrangements were made to use it temporarily for the purpose of training prospective skippers; the *Ard Casta* was issued to Ernie O'Drisceoil, Inis Cleire, Co Cork in 1957; and the *Ard Chluain* was commissioned to Louis Graham, An Daingean, Co Chiarrai in 1959.

Clearly a number of 56-footers outside the Fior-Gaeltacht Scheme were issued from 1957 onwards. While all boats issued were subject to hire purchase payment arrangements, owners who did not qualify for participation in the Fior-Gaeltacht Scheme were required to furnish an initial deposit.

By the end of 1960, apart from the five boats already dealt with, nineteen BIM 56-footers had left BIM and Tyrrells boatyards. Seven vessels were built at the BIM Killybegs yard, six at the BIM Meevagh yard, and six at the Yard of John Tyrrell & Sons, Arklow. That all BIM 56-footers were not identical is beyond dispute. Differences did exist in detail, layout, and even design. Yet, it has to be said the boats were readily recognisable, regardless of variations, which in the larger scheme of things were not that great anyway. There are I'm sure people will not agree with the latter comment! I have been asked to make it clear that Tyrrells designed their own 56-footers, and indeed 50-footers, all of which were ordered by BIM.

Throughout the 1960s further 56-footers continued to roll down the slipways of BIM boatyards. The Killybegs yard accounted for seven, culminating with the *Connacht Ranger* in 1970. Meanwhile the *Ard Eireann* and *Ard Beara* were built at Baltimore.

A Step Up

Meevagh continued with its building programme resulting in four vessels sailing away from the north Donegal coast boatyard, and at Dingle the *Guiding Star* and *Favourite* were launched. Thirty nine vessels in all! Over the period May 1956 to December 1971, the issue price increased from £12,000 to £46,823, i.e. issue price of *Ard Macha* £12,000, that of the *Favourite* £46,823.

I'm not in a position to comment on how successful the 56-footers as a whole proved to be financially. I suspect it was a mixed bag with some doing very well indeed. The BIM Annual Reports for year ended March 31st 1961 didn't reflect well on the performance of the five Gaeltacht Scheme boats, i.e. the total of 56-footers issued under the scheme).

It read as follows, "There were no additions in 1960/61 to the fleet of five 56'6" vessels operating under the provisions of the Gaeltacht Scheme. The total amount realised for catches in the year was £24,216 compared with £23,652 in 1959/60. After providing for all charges, including depreciation, there was a loss of £7,476 compared with £9,064 for 1959/60. Taking into account the deficit brought forward from previous years the balance carried forward amounts to £26,196."

It would appear that based on the above figures, one has to conclude that the boats were not paying their way.

Another statistic from the same Report that makes unsatisfactory reading is that despite continued growth in terms of numbers of vessels (50 & 56-footers) and the size increase and potential of the fleet as a whole, the weight and value of fish landed was smaller in 1960/61 than it was in 1955/56. The 1955/56 stats read 157,528 cwts (£508,233), while the 1960/61 read 121,091 cwts (497,164). It's hard to make sense of it!!

One item that appears on the BIM Annul Report for the year ending 31st March 1959 and may have had some bearing on decreased landings as recorded by the Bord, appears under the heading, Hire Purchase Landings. It reads as follows, "*Following representations made on behalf of fishermen, wholesalers, and auctioneers the Bord agreed for a trial period of six months to suspend the clause in Boat hire purchase agreements which provided that hire purchasers were bound to hand over their catches for disposal by, or at the direction of, the Board and consequently to grant to purchasers who applied for it, permission to dispose of their fish, under certain conditions ,otherwise than through the agency of the Bord. The number of fishermen who availed themselves of this concession, put into effect in October 1958, was small up to 31st March 1959.*"

A Step Up

So what is the verdict on the BIM 56-footers as boats? I think it's safe to say that a majority agree they were well-built, efficient, and for the most part well suitable for purpose when introduced in the mid-1950s. As one man remarked, "At the time they were 'small big boats'." That they were first class weather boat is also the general consensus. As a step up in many ways from their predecessors, the BIM 50-footer, one could consider them as another link in the chain. Yet, I'd have to say there are divided opinions as to how well they met requirements of era. Areas of dissatisfaction expressed by some, centre on inadequate engine power, slow and often late delivery by yards, and increases on original issue prices agreed. Comments from those who owned and fished on the boats will be later addressed.

All BIM 56-footers have more or less common origins. For the most part they were built at boatyards from the drawings of Naval Architect, James Stafford. However, I'm obliged to again point out that boats built at Tyrrell's Yard for BIM were Tyrrell designed boats. Regardless of origin, once the boats left their respective building yards and entered the world of commercial fishing, their destinies were to vary greatly. As far as I can ascertain, of the thirty-nine 56-footers built all had multiple owners, with two exceptions, Gregory Conneely's *Connacht Ranger* (G47) and *Ard Aengus,* boats built at the Mevagh Boatyard. A very close runner-up is the *Ard Casta* (D321), built at the Crosshaven Boatyard in 1957, and apart from the first few months of her earliest existence has been owned throughout by the Sheehan family, Cape Clear. Also, with only two owners is the *Ard Fionnbarr* (D370), though the time period between the owners is somewhat greater than that in the case of the *Ard Casta*. She passed from Michael Flannery, Dingle to Paddy Casey, Portmagee, and is currently owned and fished by his brother Johnny. At the other end of the scale, several boats changed hands up to seven times, possibly eight times in one or two cases.

Part I

A Step Up

Observations and Memories

Recorded here are various pieces of interesting information that came through during my research. For convenience of the reader, comments etc. are recorded under the names of the boats involved.

Ard Beara (D462)

Perhaps the most commented upon escapade of a BIM 56-footer is a passage made by the *Ard Beara* through the Dursey Sound on a December night in 1968. Weather was atrocious! In a raging storm and in turbulent conditions cascading water resulting from wind over sea reduced visibility to virtually zero. Yet, the *Ard Beara* with decks constantly awash and occasionally submerged performed away beyond the expectations of experienced seamen on board. The tragic circumstances which led to brave Castletownbere men, including the late Paddy Harrington, skipper and owner of the boat, putting to sea, has left an indelible mark on the memories of many. Word had come through that the crew of a fellow Castletownbere boat, *Sea Flower*, desperately needed rescuing from their boat which had struck a rock in Kenmare Bay. Sadly, in spite of the legendry attempt by those who manned the *Ard Beara*, the *Sea Flower* foundered. All five men on her perished!

The latter years of the *Ard Beara's* existence were spent rather ignominiously in a state of semi dereliction lying against a pier at Arthurstown, Co Wexford. What a sad sight! There were the decimated remains of a boat so highly thought of in her heyday! In her cheerless presence I closed my eyes and tried to envisage her ploughing a way through all the nastiness the Dursey Sound could throw at her. Crossing my mind too was the transient nature of life, both animate and inanimate.

In January 2011 a bulldozer and demolition equipment arrived at Arthurstown pier and put her out of her misery. In a matter of weeks evidence that the *Ard Beara* had ever existed was obliterated.

Dismantling the *Ard Beara* at Arthurstown - 2011. Credit Paddy Roche

Ard Ailbhe (D198)

The thoughts and recall of Dunmore East resident Brian Crummy, one time owner of the newly built 56-footer *Ard Ailbhe* went as follows, "At the time I got her in 1961 she was actually assigned to someone else but BIM offered her to me. I really wanted to buy a second-hand Scotch boat, a number of which were for sale at knock down prices at the time. It was a situation that came about as result of a religious quandary that left boats on the west coast of Scotland without crews. However attempts by Irish fishermen to finance the purchasing of those boats ran into difficulties. High interest rates of 18% on bank loans were bordering on prohibitive, especially so when only 4% was paid on loans for deposit on newly BIM built boats, i.e. boats built at the BIM boatyards, or boats ordered by BIM and built at the boatyard of John Tyrrell & Sons Ltd. Because of a significant horse power difference between the engines fitted in Scotch boats and those in BIM boats, generally 152hp as opposed to 114hp, the Scotch boats were a more attractive proposition in terms of fish catching potential. There are various conclusions to be drawn regarding the large discrepancies in interest rates; for instance could it have been politically motivated and linked with a ply to keep BIM boatyards in business. Regardless of the reasons, Brian still resents the prohibitive interest rate that really prevented him from buying a Scotch boat with greater fish catching potential at less than half the price he paid for the *Ard Ailbhe*.

He has a few other bones of contention regarding BIM at that time, one is that he believes the cost of boats to the fishermen at the time was artificially high – it was claimed by the proprietor of a prestigious Irish boatyard that he could build and sell boats at a much lower cost than the BIM asking price, but he was advised by the *powers that be* not to do so. Further points with which he took issue were, that having paid close to £20,000 for the boat he wasn't permitted to choose its name or the colour. As to the name he was obliged to select from one of three, each beginning with the word *Ard*. By the mid-1960s Brian was in a position to look around for boat in keeping with his original aspiration. He homed in on the 63ft *Nordkap* (D119), a 230hp Norwegian built vessel.

Brian believes it is no accident that the several among those who went on to become Ireland's most successful fishermen did not set out on the journey as BIM boat owners. On hindsight he believes that in the long run the advantages of buying a more powerful boat even at the higher rate of interest on loans outstripped the BIM boat option.

Since comments made by Michael Tyrell, a member of the illustrious boat building Tyrrell family at Arklow, seem to concur with remarks made by Brian Crummy, I thought this might be an appropriate juncture to insert them. I got the distinct impression that he was very much in agreement with what Brian Crummy had said regarding the artificially high purchase cost of boats imposed by BIM. This is part of what he had to say, "Tyrrells designed their own 56-footers (and 50-footers), boats which were *ordered* by BIM on behalf of any fishermen whom they could not persuade, financially or otherwise to order from themselves."

There were six 'BIM 56-footers' built at Tyrrell's Boatyard. Issued in 1957 were the *Glendalough* (D310) and the *Glenmalure* (D147). Two years later the *Sancta Lucia* (D4) and the *Naomh Brendain* (D76) slipped out of the yard. Not by any means resting on their laurels the Arklow shipwrights were on cue with two further boats ready for delivery in 1960 – the *Ard Dallan* (D240) and the *Ard Ciaran* (311). Michael spoke of the 'load carrying' qualities of the 56-footers built at Tyrrells, "They were correctly trimmed. I saw the two Glens in Dunmore East loaded full of herring. To look across the harbour at them some people may have sensed there was something wrong. It was nothing really except that they were down about 2ft on their draft marks. They were properly trimmed; not *everybody* understood that."

Ard Carna (D328)

This is a narrative I've heard a few versions of. One sometimes has to be careful of the Chinese whispers syndrome! I believe the most reliable account of what happened to the *Ard Carna* and its crew in the early summer of 1983 is that of Tommy Ralston, then coxswain of the Mallig RNLI Lifeboat. He recalls that word filtered through that an Irish trawler (*Ard Carna*) had not been in contact with anyone for a few days, and that concern was growing for the safety of the crew. The boat had been fishing on grounds south of Tiree when last heard of. The Mallig Lifeboat was searching the area in perfect weather conditions when an aircraft that was also searching made VHF contact with the missing boat. The message from the aircraft to the controlling Coastguard was that a weak signal had been picked up. It had however been established that the crew were well but suffering badly from a shortage of cigarettes!

So how or why did the *Ard Carna* go missing? Well it appears that the skipper decided to change fishing grounds. In the course of doing so the boat was making a night passage when a metal pipe connecting two fuel tanks ruptured. As a result the entire fuel supply began to leak into the bilges. To enhance the safety of the boat at sea a bilge alarm had been fitted a short time previously. With level of liquid rising, the alarm alerted the bilge pump and it duly responded by pumping out any liquid that came its way. Unfortunately the pump wasn't to know that it was slowly but surely emptying the contents of both fuel tanks into the sea. With an unsuspecting crew unaware of what was happening, the engine eventually stopped because of lack of fuel. The boat was then powerless and well out of reach of stations using the short-range VHF. In an easterly breeze the helpless *Ard Carna* was slowly making her way westwards into great expanses of the Atlantic Ocean! However, thanks to the vigilant aircraft observer her position was passed on to a rescue vessel. To the relief of all concerned the boat was towed back to port where I'm told business at the local tobacconists was immediately brisk. The incident caused quite a stir at the time with concern for the missing boat and its crew growing by the day.

The *Ard Carna* at Castletownbere. Credit Tony Muldoon.

St Bernadette (D57), Ard Colm (D37), Ard Aengus (?), Ard Rathain (D262), Connacht Ranger (G47), Ard Chluain (D349) and Ard Scia (D55)

The death of Aran Island's iconic fisherman, skipper and fleet owner, Gregory Conneelly, sent shockwaves through the Irish fishing community. It seemed almost unbelievable! When I spoke to him on the phone in October 2011 he had just being watching one of the Presidential debates on television; he would be voting for 'the local man'! Little did I think that the intended visit to meet up with Gregory on the Aran Islands in the summer 2012 was not to be! Yes, at his home on February 12th, following a short illness, he sadly passed away. Initially, it was hard to take in that he would not be seen on Kilronan pier again!

One of those people singled out for greatness, Gregory with a talent for stone masonry and carpentry built his own house at 18 years of age. When there was little work on the Island for young men in the early 1950s, Gregory crewed for some years on trawlers operating out of Milford Haven. Later when back home in the Aran Islands he embarked on the first Skipper Training Programme ever organised by the Department of Land and Fisheries and administered by An Bord Iascaigh Mhara. He successfully completed the training and was awarded a *Second Hand Special Certificate* in 1959 – one of the first such certificates to be issued to Irish fishermen – I believe it might have been the second.

When fishing out of Howth on Gerry O'Shea's *St Bernadette* in 1961 he tragically lost a leg in an accident off the Rockabill Lighthouse. It was not in the man's nature to quit easily, and in this instance showed his resilience by later returning to fishing as skipper of the BIM owned *Ard Colm*, a boat his brother John later bought. In 1964 Gregory had the *Ard Aengus* built at Mevagh. Through misadventure she was lost off the Aran Islands four years later. Gregory who was not on board at the time went to the scene in the *Ard Colm*, and in what has been described as 'a terrific feat of seamanship' saved the crew of the *Ard Aengus* before she broke up in heavy seas.

Again Gregory showed his resilience when in 1969, three months following the loss of the *Ard Aengus,* he bought the *Ard Rathain* from BIM. One year later he became owner of the brand new 56-footer, *Connacht Ranger*! It would appear that Gregory had a great affinity for BIM 56-footers because in 1972 he became owner of yet another one, the *Ard Chluain*.

Throughout the 1960s and 1970s and into the 1980s, Gregory was a main mover in all that went on in west coast fishing. Stepping up from the 56-footers he had the 80ft *Fort Aengus* (G4) built at Killybegs in 1975. Umpteen young men who later went on to become high profile fishermen learned their trade on the decks and wheelhouses of Gregory's multiple boats. Ashore, he was well recognised for his input to furthering the causes of the local fishing industry, and not least his involvement in the establishment of the Galway and Aran Fishermen's Co-operative in 1975, an organisation of which he remained chairman for many years. It was as result of pressure from Gregory and men of similar calibre that saw new harbours built at Rossaveal, Co Galway and at Kilronan on the Aran Island of Inis Mor.

Along with a group of other trawlers, some local, some visitors, he was also instrumental in establishing prawn trawling for the first time off the west coast. Skerries man, Peter Campbell, skipper and owner of the *Ard Gillen* and one of those involved, had this to say, "A few of us who had experience of prawn fishing on the east coast led the pack, but local knowledge provided by Gregory Conneely and Kieran Gill was invaluable. It was a case of both factions liaising closely. It worked well."He went on to say, "I recall the *Connacht Ranger* and Kieran Gill's *Ard Scia* making very big landings. Also during door trawling Gregory's *Ard Chluain* caught huge amounts of fish."

A Step Up

Indeed Gregory was a man of many talents, too numerous to record here. Above all though, he will be remembered as a fisherman supreme. A few years ago in general conversation with the now late Gerry O'Shea, Howth, on whose boats Gregory fished in the early 1960s, he remarked to me on how fortunate he was to have had great crews over the years. He went on to name a few, individuals who later excelled in the world of fishing, but interestingly, the first mentioned was Gregory, followed by Kevin McHugh, Willie Devanney, Mick Doyle and his own brother Teddy. An early indication of the competence of the great man!

The *Connacht Ranger* and *Ard Chluain* at Kilronan. Credit M.Conneely.

Girl Eileen (D13)

Killybegs man, Pat Moore, recalls an incident that took place when he fished on his uncle Mossey's *Girl Eileen*. It happened in Clew Bay, Co Mayo. While the incident had potential for serious consequences, Pat in relating the story made light of it, and indeed added the occasional amusing anecdote. It went as follows, "There was the night on the *Girl Eileen*. It was one of the years we were down in Achill herring ringing. The three Moore family owned boats were there. I was on the *Girl Eileen* with my uncle Mossey, my father Martin was on the *Vigilant* and my uncle Benny was on the *Brothers Hope*. One night as the weather deteriorated the wind went around to the south west. We decided to move south and take shelter behind Clare Island in the mouth of Clew Bay. Having dropped anchor the crew of the *Girl Eileen* went 'below' to play cards. There was a chap keeping an eye out in the wheelhouse but somehow unnoticed by him the wind quickly changed around to the north, the anchor chain broke and the next thing we knew the boat had been thrown onto rocks and was lying on her side. Panic broke out! I wasn't all that worried, I was a good swimmer and white breaking water visible along the shoreline meant that we weren't too far off. Strange the things that enter your mind at times like that – I remembered that I had a ten shilling note under the mattress and off I went down to the cabin to retrieve it. That was my priority! I still remember that there was considerable panic on desk with the crew trying to balance and stay upright. No one knew what was going to happen next! What did happen was that a big wave came along and washed the boat off the reef. By then the men in the other two boats were aware of our mishap and were standing by to help. The *Vigilant* came alongside and took some crew off the *Girl Eileen*. Mossey, myself and one other chap stayed aboard. That the underside of the boat had been damaged soon became evident as the water level inside rose. While Mossey steered her up through the islands and on into Westport constant pumping out took place. From there we arranged for shipwrights to come from the Killybegs boatyard to access the damage. It transpired that there was keel and planking damage but that temporary repair work could be carried out there and then. We continued to fish for another couple of weeks before returning home. Apparently the long trip back to Killybegs in the damaged boat that required regular pumping out didn't appeal to some crew members who concocted half baked reasons for travelling by other means." Again Pat laughed as he recalled crew members jumping in trepidation from the *Girl Eileen* onto the *Vigilant* in the darkness of Clew Bay. He believes that had there been long jump Olympic gold medals on offer they would have won hands down.

Something completely different came up during my chat with Pat, and it was something that surprised me a little, it was his observation on the load carrying capabilities of the *Girl Eileen*. He reckoned, "She wasn't especially good," and went on to quote instances when not particularly overloaded, of seeing the sea coming in through hawse pipes and flowing back along the deck, she was he said, "Nearly like a submarine."

The *Girl Eileen*. Photographer unknown.

Ard Fionnbarr (D402), St Catherine (D299, Ard Casta (D321), Ard Carna (D328), Ard Eireann (D106) and Favourite (SO351)

At the time of writing, as far as I can ascertain, the *Ard Fionnbarr* and the *St Catherine* are the only remaining 56-footers actively engaged in fishing. For one reason or another, the 'new' Code of Practice, introduced in 2009 impinged greatly on the prospects of other well maintained boats having a future in fishing. The *Ard Casta, Ard Carna and Ard Eireann* are prime examples. Indeed the fine condition of the *Ard Casta* hasn't gone unnoticed on the south coast, because at Baltimore Seafood and Traditional Wooden Boat Festival in May 2012, plaques painted by traditional wooden boat enthusiast Nigel Towse, and John Simpson, honoured the vessel which was described thus, "A wonderfully maintained example of a traditional wooden trawler." In 2011 another BIM 56-footer to hit the dust where commercial fishing is concerned is the *Favourite*, the last one to be built. Having considered the pros and cons of investing fairly heavily in bringing her up to the required Code of Practice standard, owners Jason and Stevie Moore, Killybegs decided not to proceed with the work.

Immense credit goes to the O'Gorman family, Achill Island, owners of the *St Catherine*, and to the Casey family, Portmagee, Co Kerry for looking after their boats so well down through the years. While some updating was necessary in the fields of tracking systems, and, health and safety, only minimal work was otherwise required to ensure that both vessels successfully passed the Code of Practice.

The *Ard Fionnbarr*, whose only previous owner was Michael Flannery, Dingle, was originally fished by Johnny and his brother Patie. Patie later bought another boat. The *Ard Fionnbarr* is currently owned and fished by Johnny, a mild mannered and unassuming man well known to all who frequent Portmagee.

The *St Catherine*, whose only previous owner was Seamus Murrin, Killybegs, was successfully fished for many years by Michael O'Gorman. When Michael retired he left the boat in the very capable hands of his two sons, James and Mickey. Now working from Cloughmore, Achill Island they land crayfish, lobster and white fish at the port. The fruits of their labours can be sampled in Achill during the summer months by purchasing from the very highly rated O'Gorman family fish shop.

Long may the Ard Fionnbarr and St Catherine endure!

The *Ard Eireann* moored in Schull harbour – 2010. Credit Paddy Roche

The *Ard Fionnbarr* at Portmagee – 2010.Credit Paddy Roche.

St Bernadette (D57)

Gerry O'Shea, who originally hailed from the Castletownbere area of Co Cork, was first owner of the *St Bernadette*. In 1958 Gerry's BIM 50-footer, *Ros Beara,* was out of commission as result of a collision involving another boat at Dunmore East. While lengthy repairs were being carried out Gerry needed a boat and not being one to hang around he approached BIM regarding a 56-footer that he knew was lying unallocated at Mevagh Boatyard. That boat was the *St Bernadette*.

In the early 1960s Gerry moved on and purchase larger boats, including 'beamers'. During those years the *St Bernadette* was put up for sale. There were no immediate takers! Rather than having her tied up at Howth, Gerry suggested to his brother Teddy, who had recently acquired a skipper's ticket, that he should begin fishing her. So he did, at first out of Howth before moving to Killybegs. Accompanying him as crew was his sixteen year old brother Pierce, Mick Doyle and Kevin McHugh. It time Teddy got his own boat, the *Charlotte Chambers*, the *St Bernadette* was sold on, and his crew went their separate ways.

As a point of interest, during my meeting with Gerry he reflected back to the young man from Redcross, Co Wicklow who came to him looking for a berth on his then boat, the *Primula*. He had no fishing background but Gerry took him on anyway. That young man was Mick Doyle who went on to become one of Ireland's top fishermen, boat owner and businessman.

Later another teenager joined Gerry's *Primula*. He was a virtually unknown young man from Achill Island, Co Mayo, who in the first instance came as an apprentice to fish on Willie Reynold's BIM 50-footer *Eiscir Riada* at Balbriggan. That young man was Kevin McHugh!

From humble beginnings on the *Primula* and the *St Bernadette,* the names of Teddy, Mick and Kevin were to become bywords in fishing circles, and were destined to make an indelible impact on the Irish fishing industry.

On Monday July 23rd 2012 I received a telephone call from Gerry's wife, Mary. The words that came to my ear saddened me greatly, "Pat, I'm ringing to tell you that Gerry was buried last Friday." My mind flicked back to the fine young man who fished the *Ros Beara* in Kenmare Bay all those years ago, and then to the elderly gentleman I met at Howth more recently. During the in-between years, as forward looking men in fishing go, Gerry was king, and indeed he was the daddy of skippers when it came to training up crew. A tough but fair man! A great, great fisherman! May he rest in peace!

The *St Bernadette* (D57) at Castletownbere –late 1950s. Photo via BIM

Ard Scia (D55), Ard Rathain (D262) and Connacht Ranger (G47)

The Ard Scia is a boat fondly remembered in the Aran Islands! A tribute to her late original owner, Kieran Gill, penned by Olwen Gill, exemplify the affection in which the boat and owner were held by all fortunate enough to have known them. Kieran began his fishing career as a fourteen year old deckhand on one of the boats fished by the renowned Thompson brothers, Willie, George and Jimmy. Hailing from Lossiemouth, Scotland, the brothers have been widely credited with heralding a new era in fishing on the southern Irish coast in the 1940s and early '50s. Some years later Kieran took charge of the 56-footer *Ard Rathain*, but it is from 1966 onwards, his years of ownership and skippering the *Ard Scia* that he is best remembered. The *Ard Scia* and Gregory Conneely's *Connacht Ranger*, also a BIM 56-footer, made a notable pair-fishing combination in the early 1970s, landing huge amounts of fish first at Galway and later at Rossaveal. A deckhand on the *Ard Scia* during those years remembers regular white fish landing of hundreds of boxes.

A Step Up

That the *Ard Scia*, or '*The Scia'*, as she was locally known, meant more than a fishing boat to past generations of Aran Island folk, has not been forgotten. Over the years, under the guiding hand of the ever so generous and good natured Kieran, cargo, including food, fuel and furniture were transported from mainland to the island free gratis and for nothing. The quite, religious man described as having a great sense of humour and a smile on his face for everyone sadly passed away at the age of 56 in 1992.

The *Ard Scia* spent all her working days on the west coast. When the inevitable ending came along it was executed via dismantling and demolition at Rossaveal.

Undergoing demolition - the *Ard Scia* berthed beside the *Westward Isle* at Rossaveal. Photo via *Marine Times*

Ard Gillen (D453), Connacht Ranger (G47), Ard Scia (D55) and Ard Chluain (D349)

Retired Skerries fisherman, Peter Campbell, was one time owner of the *Ard Gillen.* In 1976 he bought her from the Fergusons, one of the best known fishing families on the east coast. He has a philosophy that modern day trawling had its roots in the BIM 56-footers. He purchased the *Ard Gillen* at a time when the herring boom had ended. Just then many experienced fishermen couldn't see beyond the 50-footers where trawling was concerned. That perception was based on very real economic reasoning – larger boats were going to be more expensive to run at a time when the fishing industry as a whole was far from flourishing. How were larger boats engaged in trawling going to generate enough money to make them feasible? They were simply too expensive run! Peter is in no doubt that during the 1970s and possibly the early 1980s 65ft whitefish boats of trawling out of Skerries couldn't pay their way. There was plenty of fish to be caught but market prices were poor. However, if progress was to be made where trawling was concerned then efficient 'small big boats', i.e. boats larger than 50-footers but smaller than 65 or 70-footers were seen as the way forward. The 56-footers fitted the bill. They raised the trawling potential of boats up a notch by being excellent sea boats and not overly expensive to operate. At the same time they had the capability of catching huge amounts of fish – "It took time, but the upsurge in modern trawling initiated by the 56-footers in the 1970s, and that gradually gained momentum over the years, led to incremental increases in timber boat sizes, and to the modern steel hulled trawlers of today."

Peter began fishing the *Ard Gillen* off the east coast. We had, he said, "Some great landings of cod in those early years; we recorded hauls of over one hundred boxes." In 1980 he moved to the west coast, where along with other 56-footer teams he began springtime pair-trawling in Galway Bay with John F. Lynch's 52ft, Norwegian built *Marita (G1).* That same year his *Ard Gillen* along with a group of six or so other boats, some locals and some visitors, broke new ground by delving into the world of prawn trawling off the west coast for the first time. He recalls that Gregory Conneely's *Connacht Ranger* and Kieran Gill's *Ard Scia,* both BIM 56-footers, were involved. Because of their size 56-footers were economically suitable for prawn fishing. Peter went on to say, "Those of us who had experienced prawn fishing on the east coast led the pack. Local knowledge provided by men such as Kieran and Gregory was invaluable. It was a case of both factions liaising closely. It worked out very well. That's when commercial prawn fishing off the Galway coast began. The first year, in a matter of a few months, there was £56,000 pounds worth of prawns landed. I predicted that figure would hit the £1,000,000 very quickly, and a few years later it did so. In those years through pair-trawling and working with doors we also recorded high landings of whitefish. Commonplace was hauls of two hundred boxes of mixed whitefish when pairing. Other boats I recall making very high landings were the *Connacht Ranger* and the *Ard Scia.* Also while door- trawling Gregory's *Ard Chluain* landed huge amounts of fish. Whiting made up the bulk of pair-fishing catches. Marketing whiting was frequently problematic and as such led to fishing not always being financially viable. To overcome the problem one particular season I decided to break up the partnership arrangement and take up single-boat trawling. In that way I was able to target better quality fish and at the same time fish for whiting when the market was good. When we first started inshore trawling off Galway with the *Ard Gillen* new pieces of ground found yielded an abundance of high quality fish. Some of the first clear hauls we made still stick in my mind; a three hour tow on one occasion produced eleven boxes of monk, ten boxes of megrims, a box of jumbo prawns and three boxes of mixed other fish. It was bordering on phenomenal when you think about it – nearly half a ton of monk, hard to understand it now. For a day's fishing we occasionally landed up to two hundred boxes of trawl fish. It's was indeed something else."

With a job well done by both skipper and vessel, Peter in 1983 decided the time was right to raise the profile of his fishing career to another level and engage in deepwater prawn and whitefish trawling. As such the Ard Gillen was sold in order to make way for the 82ft *Iuda Naofa.* He still believes the 56-footers and especially his own *Ard Gillen* was a bit special.

The *Ard Gillen* at Arklow – 2006. Credit P.Nolan.

Ard Finnian (D402), Ard Rathain (D262), Ard Mhuire (D5), and Ard Gillen (D453)

A man with an apparent affinity for BIM 56-footers is Seamus Corr, Skerries, Co Dublin. Between solo ownership, and in partnership with his brother Frank, he skippered no less than three of the great boats. When I met up with Seamus he was initially keen to recall his early years of fishing out of Loughshinney in the family owned BIM 50-footer *Ros Sean*. She was at the time (1955/'56), he said, "A beautiful state-of-the-art Mevagh built varnished hulled boat. Her arrival at Loughshinney caused a great stir in the local community. People were up and down to the pier all day long too see the new boat and many went on board to look the vessel over. So enthralled was my ninety year old grandfather with the cabin and its comforts that he just wanted to stay on board. He was refusing to go home for his dinner! Nowadays million pound boats arrive at ports virtually unnoticed. How times have changed!"

Seamus has great memories of his years on the *Ros Sean* when skippered by Georgie Corr. "We did very well, though we had the occasional disappointment." He recalled one particular trip to Morecombe Bay which had amusing aspects to it. He described the 'adventure' as follows, "I was still young and the older men were in charge. Other local boats were fishing in the Bay so we set off to join them not knowing exactly where we were going. None of the crew had fished there previously. The sum total of navigational aids aboard was a compass. I'm not sure how long we were at sea but myself and another young chap, Stephen Attley, (later owner of the 56-footer *Morning Star*) were down in the cabin when a call came from the skipper to come up as it was time to shoot. I asked Georgie how he knew we were at the fishing grounds, to which he replied, I don't know but I can see John Henry (Doyle) in the *Conquest* over there, so we must be in the right place.

Another member of the Corr clan, Eddie, had made special tail ends of about 100mm mesh for the trawl. Having shot the net Stephen and I returned to the cabin. Ten or fifteen minutes later Georgie again called for us to come on deck. The trawl has to be foul of rocks or something I thought to myself, it's nowhere near long enough shot! When we asked what was wrong the skipper said he wasn't sure but there was something amiss. Being on an unknown fishing ground he felt that we should attempt to board the net. That we did! To our amazement the tail end was full of massive plaice! With our hands ripped to pieces from handling fish from the first and subsequent hauls we headed for home with 250 boxes of the finest plaice you ever saw." Alas, there ended the happy part of the story because a glut of plaice in the Dublin market meant that the fish failed to find a buyer – they were dumped. Instead of a lucrative return for the boat load of prime fish, the owner, my uncle Jack (Corr), received a bill for expenses incurred. He personally delivered the bad news to us and in way of lessening the blow gave us each £20 out of his own pocket."

Following his years on the *Ros Sean,* Seamus was in a position to invest in his own boat. He looked around for a suitable vessel. On the market was the *Ard Finnian*, a BIM 56-footer, built at the Killybegs Yard in 1962. Having been re-engined and in good condition, "a lovely little boat," Seamus purchased her in 1972. Now, all these years later, the recalling of his purchase reminded him to tell me of the very first time he saw the *Ard Finnian*. "We were fishing outside the Rockabill (in the *Ros Sean* I presume) and there fishing beside us was this 'beauty' with a mizzen set. She was owned by Paddy Sugrue, a Kerryman, who then fished out of Howth. As we feasted our eyes on this beautiful boat, the older men on the crew came to the conclusion that she was too big for fishing locally. How times have changed! If only they could see the boats trawling there now, massive boats up to 120ft in length!"

Immediately following the acquisition of the *Ard Finnian,* Seamus engaged in seine netting for six months or so. Then he changed over to prawn trawling and that particular fishing was to be the main stay for the remainder of his career. He recalled that in those days cod were very plentiful in the spring of the year. Where the cod later disappeared to is another story!

Things had gone well for Seamus! He decided to move up to a bigger boat! It was a decision that in 1976 led to the purchased of the brand new 65ft *Francis Maria.* Unfortunately his venture coincided with the closure of the Celtic Sea herring fishery and poor prawn prices. He was having difficulty making her pay and believes he was fortunate to meet up with interested buyers – "Well established fishermen Frank and Joe Doherty, Kincasslagh, Co Donegal."

With the *Francis Maria* gone Seamus fished on a local boat, the *Carnown Bay*, for some months while keeping an eye out for a suitable boat to come on the market. His quest took him to Howth where on the advice of one John Dixon, an elderly shipwright, he became interested in a particular BIM 56-footer, the *Ard Rathain.* Fitted with a brand new Gardner engine, the 1956 Mevagh built boat was in great condition – "a grand little boat." Was she up for sale or not? At first her owner, Baltimore man Pat Harrington seemed uncertain! However Seamus along with his brother Frank decided to pursue the matter. Frank rang Pat who after some hesitation decided to sell the boat. All of that took place in 1979, the year Seamus and Frank became owners of the *Ard Rathain.*

During the years Seamus fished the *Ard Rathain* he had some memorable catches of cod. A great man to recall, he reflected on one such landing in 1980. The story went, "I love horse racing, so my wife Olivia and I went to Fairy House for the Irish Grand National one Easter Monday. I believe that during the course of the day, and night, I over indulged in the hard stuff, so much so that I wasn't feeling at all well the following morning! Going to sea had very little appeal on that particular Tuesday. However, old habits die hard so where else would one go to see what was happening but to the pier and perhaps a visit to Joe Mays (the local). By then it was then around 10am. Some boats had already headed off to the fishing grounds. I must have been coming around a bit at that stage, or maybe I was feeling a little guilty, but for whatever reason I decided to go too. While the other boats were fishing to the east I went north towards where I could see a single boat. It turned out to be the smashing Tyrrell built, 70ft *Shelmalier* (WD63). Floating alongside her was an enormous bag of cod waiting to be boarded. I immediately got on 'the blower' and informed the skippers of other Skerries boats that it looked as if cod were on the go. Some believed I was just joking, but Peter Campbell, skipper of the *Ard Gillen* decided there was some truth in what I was telling them and headed towards us.

At the same time we came across the *Tom Tom Louis* (D488), skippered by Paddy Mc Grath, heading for Howth and down to the numbers. He had been fishing over the weekend. We went on and picked up the spot where the cod were. The sounder went black! We shot a prawn net and towed through the marking. When it came up it was balloon like – 180 boxes of cod and 20 boxes of whiting! Peter, likewise, who had also shot at that stage, boarded around 200 boxes. A second shot yielded us a further 140 boxes. Peter had something similar. The two boats, *Ard Rathain* and *Ard Gillen*, were filled from stem to stern with cod. Fortunately the sea was as smooth as glass as we made our way back to Skerries. Otherwise the fish would have fallen out over the rails. Between the two 56-footers we landed over 700 boxes, mostly of cod, and all caught in prawn nets. It was almost unbelievable! The following day there wasn't a cod to be caught in the same spot. A huge shoal must have come in to spawn on the soft bottom. Most of the cod caught were females. Unfortunately once again poor prices at the Dublin market took much of the gloss off the landings. We got little or nothing for them; the absence of worthwhile markets at the time meant rock bottom prices. Occasionally fish completely failed to sell. It happened at a time when up to eight lorry loads of fish, mostly whiting, left Skerries pier four or five nights a week for the Dublin market."

As the years moved on the *Ard Rathain* was sold to Dick Deasy, Union Hall. There was then a short interlude in the Corr fishing activities before they once again began to look around for another boat. This time they settled for the 1960, Scotch built, 55-footer, *Boy Stephen* (D656). She was bought from a Kilkeel owner. The Corrs replaced the 114hp Gardner fitted, with a 280hp/209kW Volvo Penta. She was a fine boat that served the Corr family well before once again selling her on to Dick Deasy.

Following the now almost customary interlude between selling and buying boats, circa 1988 the Corrs decided on yet another BIM 56-footer. The 1958, Mevagh built *Ard*

Mhuire (D5) was to be the third of that particular breed skippered by Seamus. She was purchased from Michael Doherty, Greencastle, and was to prove a very successful boat. Seamus said, "We did well with her, very well. We fished her for fifteen years. By then she was getting long in the tooth." While the *Ard Mhuire* ended her days in Skerries Seamus still has a few lasting memories of her. There is one particular incident that surpasses all others; one that he will never forget. He described the pertinent happening as follows, "We were hauling the trawl one nasty, dirty day. My youngest son James was standing near the rail. The boat was rolling and tossing and as the net came up the chain snapped hitting James and causing him to overbalance. He fell overboard! It all happened so quickly that it took an instant to realise what had gone on. The boat had drifted ahead. Then I saw James in the water! Looking towards him I could see he was trying to swim to the boat. We closed in on him, but try as we might, with a big swell causing the boat to lift and fall irregularly, water splashing all over the place, and interfering pieces of gear getting in the way, we could not get him out of the water. Fortunately one of the Irish Navy vessels was nearby and came to the rescue. A boarding dingy was quickly launched and headed for James whom the crew lifted from the water. He was taken to the Navy vessel and later landed in Skerries none the worse for the ordeal. I will never forget the agony of those minutes James was in the water and of our helplessness in not being able to get him back on board. It makes me tremble to think about it to this day. Had I lost the boy I would never again have put my foot on a boat."

With the *Ard Mhuire* now in retirement the Corrs turned their attention to a bigger boat, the *Adastra* (G485). They purchased her from Bertie Ahern, not the ex Taoiseach as I momentarily concluded, but a man of the same name from the Aran Islands. By then the new century was well and truly established. With it came a term, Code of Practice, which was to have far reaching implications for many fishermen and their boats. The Corr's experienced those particular implications in the early days of *Adastra* ownership by 'putting her through at the time'. Having fished her for three-and-a-half years, what Seamus describes as 'the more serious Code of Practice', came into being (2009). It was decision time – should they or shouldn't they go ahead with a survey? It was going to be costly! They went ahead with it anyway. The outcome was that a major keel job would be required and the 230hp Gardner engine also needed attention. Seamus and Frank were no longer young men. There would be a lot of expense involved! In the final analysis it wasn't feasible to invest further money in the boat. At the time of writing the *Adastra* was permanently tied up at Skerries pier.

Now, could it be that the very long fishing tradition established by generation after generation of the Corr family was about to come to an end? The answer to that question is no! With the *Asrtada* tied up Seamus and his son, James, kept an eye out for another boat! In time word filtered through that a suitable vessel might be coming up for sale. It came about when the O'Flaherty's (Kilmore Quay) bought a steel hulled

48ft trawler named *Our Tracey*. She was in fact too small for their business and had made the purchase in order to procure a scallop licence that went with her. With the boat lying in Howth, Seamus suggested to James that he should go and look her over. Satisfied that she was what he wanted, James spoke to Denis O'Flaherty and a deal was done. She arrived at Skerries in February 2012. With her name changed to the *Sheriff* (Seamus' nickname of many years), skippered by James, and with his brother Frank (Francis) on the crew, she was engaged in prawn fishing when I called at the Corr home in May 2012. Seamus is obviously overjoyed that James has carried on the family fishing tradition. He is equally pleased that James' older brother Frank, who having done his skippers ticket, went on to spent some years working as a chef, has now come back to make his living as a fisherman. Satisfaction too is derived from the fact that cousin, Georgie Corr, fishes the Price owned fishing vessel *Primrose* (DA93) out of Balbriggan. Long may the Corr family fishing tradition continue!

End of the line - The *Ard Mhuire* at Skerries. Credit John Kinsella.

Ard Colm (D37)

I've been told that the initial role of the Mevagh built *Ard Colm* was that of a training vessel for prospective skippers, and possibly fishermen in general. It appears that BIM appointed an Icelandic gentleman for the purpose of instructing local men in best fishing practices. The project, reportedly, was an abject failure with lost gear and other mishaps being an almost daily occurrence. The venture appears to have come to an abrupt end, resulting in the *Ard Colm* lying idle for a period of time before being taken over by Aran Island's Gregory Conneely. He fished her for BIM. She was later sold to his brother John, who in turn sold her to Brian Farren, Greencastle. Brian remembers John Conneely, "As a great and descent man who handed over all spare parts that went with the boat – even a propeller." This is what Brian had to say about the *Ard Colm*, "She was a fine boat in every way. She was big and strong, and a great weather boat. I remember getting caught out in exceptionally bad weather when I had to drive on hard into mountainous waves. Later I was to learn that the only water taken in came through the wheelhouse windows. There was no need for a bilge pump; she was the driest boat ever." He recalled too fishing the *Ard Colm* eighty miles off Inishowen Head in the early 1980s and getting loads of haddock. Unfortunately, poor fish prices and the ever increasing cost of diesel, led to Brian selling the boat on.

When owned by Denis Coll, Inisbofin, Co Donegal, she ran onto rocks at the mouth of Mulroy Bay, Co Donegal. Attempts to tow her off at the time failed. She later refloated of her own accord and went ashore on rocky stretch of strand on the Mulroy Bay coastline. There she was to remain![1]

Ard Dallan (D240)

The *Ard Dallan*, built in 1960, was originally owned by Joe McBride, Burtonport, Co Donegal. She is reported to have fished very successfully right through to the early 1970s, a time when the trend was for owners to invest in bigger boats. Consequently, the *Ard Dallan* was sold on and replaced by the newly built 65-foot state-of-the-art *Evelyn Marie.* The change of boats meant that the *Ard Dallan's* crew switched on to the *Evelyn Marie*. Sadly, in January 1975 the *Evelyn Marie* inexplicitly ran on to a reef and foundered at the Island of Rathlin O'Beirne off the west Donegal coast. All hands went down with her! Of the six men who perished at least five had previously fished

[1] A diver who went down to inspect the hull observed that so strong were the timbers used in the building of the boat that they had twisted rather than breaking on impact - testimony Brian Farren says, "To what a strong, well built boat she was."

on the *Ard Dallan* – they were skipper Paddy Bonner, Hughie Gallagher, Johnny O'Donnell, Roland Faughnan and Tom Ham. The sixth man who lost his life was Joe O'Donnell may also have been an *Ard Dallan* crewmember.

Part II

The Boats – The Owners – The Destinations

It is important that the following data should be read in the context of information collected from many different sources. Because the boats involved were issued between the mid-1950s and 1971, a long time ago, it has been difficult to establish a full history of each individual vessel. The main contributors have been the boat owners and those who fished in them. Unfortunately, recalling intermittent happenings over half a century ago involving people, boats, boatyards, destinations, ports, etc. can be confusing. From day one, records of boat ownership and movements, official or otherwise, do not exist. While every effort has been made to substantiate the content, it is inevitable that some inaccuracies may have arisen. For those I apologise. The establishment of chronological ownership has proved the most difficult aspect of the compilation.

Boats are listed alphabetically as follows:

1. Names beginning with Ard 1 to 22.
2. Others 23 to 39.

1. Ard Aengus (?)

Builders: BIM Boatyard Mevagh.

Year of Issue: 1964.

Original Owner: Gregory Conneely.

First Homeport: Kilronan, Aran Islands, Co Galway.

Subsequent History: Gregory fished the *Ard Aengus* until November in 1968 when she got into difficulties off the Aran Islands and eventually broke up in heavy seas. Fortunately there was no loss of life.

2. *Ard Aidhm (D378)*

Builders: BIM Boat Yard Mevagh, Co Donegal.

Year of Issue: 1961.

Original Owner: Ronan Mallon.

First Homeport: Dun Laoghaire, Co Dublin.

Subsequent History: My understanding is that *Ard Aidhm* became available to Ronan when the individual she was initially intended for had a change of mind. He fished her out of Dun Laoghaire for a few years. During her stay she was victim of considerable storm damage at Dun Laoghaire pier. Her next owner was Peter McCallig, Killybegs. In the 1970s when sold on to a K.Fraser, Saltburn, on the north-east coast of England, she was re-registered WY135. A year later she became the property of Kenneth W. Denham, in nearby Whitby. Around 1980, the partnership of Kenneth and George L Storr were the last known owners. I have been told that she was lost at sea but no details of circumstances were available.

The Ard Aidhm. Photo via The Irish Skipper

3. Ard Ailbhe (D198)

Builders: BIM Boatyard Mevagh, Co Donegal.

Year of Issue: 1960.

Original Owner: Brian Crummy.

First Homeport: Dun Laoighaire, Co Dublin.

Subsequent History: The *Ard Ailbe* remained in Brian's ownership until the mid-1960s. During that time, fishing mostly out of Dunmore East, the *Ard Ailbe* paired at different times with *Quit or Doubles* and the *Primula*, boats owned respectively by Leo Crummy (Brian's brother) and Mick Doyle. Circa 1964 Brian sold the *Ard Ailbe* to Lawrence Lett, Wexford, who in turn sold her to Liam Rossiter, Kilmore Quay. Liam fished her from Kilmore Quay until the late 1990s. Around 2000 she was broken up on the slipway at Kilmore Quay.

The Ard Ailbe. Credit Peter O'Shea.

4. Ard Aluinn (D498)

Builders: BIM Boatyard Killybegs, Co Donegal.

Year of Issue: 1968.

Original Owner: Des Faherty.

First Homeport: Kilronan, Aran Islands, Co Galway.

Subsequent History: When Des took delivery of the 80ft *Azure Sea* from the Killybegs Boatyard in December 1973 he sold the *Ard Aluinn* to Pat Connolly, Clogherhead. From Clogherhead she went to Donal O'Neill at Castletownbere. Donal subsequently sold her on to Dick Deasy, Union Hall. Her next and final move was back to Castletownbere when Jim Dan O'Sullivan purchased her from Dick.

The *Ard Aluinn* at Castletownbere. Credit Peter O'Shea.

5. Ard Beara (D462)

Builders: BIM Boatyard Baltimore, Co Cork.

Year of Issue: 1967.

Original Owner: Paddy Harrington.

First Homeport: Castletownbere, Co Cork.

Subsequent History: A much travelled boat! While in Paddy's ownership, during a raging storm she took part in failed but valiant attempted to rescue the crew of the grounded MFV *Sea Flower* in Kenmare Bay on a December night in 1968. Some years later Paddy sold the *Ard Beara* to James McLoughlin, Greencastle, Co Donegal, who in turn sold her to Dick Deasy, Union Hall. Circa three years later Anthony Sheehy, Baltimore bought her from Dick. During Anthony's ownership I understand she was variously fished by Jerry O'Driscoll, Kinsale, and Paul Hart of Clonakilty. Her next homeport was Crosshaven, Co Cork, when under the ownership of Aidan McSweeney she was fished for a short time by Pat O'Driscoll, Cape Clear. Following Pat's departure she was taken over by other skippers but eventually spent time tied up at Crosshaven before being purchased by Ger Foley, Ballyhack, Co Wexford! Latterly, she spent several years in a semi-derelict state before being broken up at Arthurstown, Co Wexford, in January 2011.

The *Ard Beara* in her latter days. Credit Paddy Roche

6. Ard Carna (D328)

Builders: BIM Boatyard Killybegs, Co Donegal.

Year of Issue: 1961.

Original Owner: Thomas Murrin.

First Homeport: Killybegs, Co Donegal.

Subsequent History: Following Thomas Murrin's ownership in the early to mid-1970s the *Ard Carna* was purchased by John Kearney, Leenankeel, Clonmany, Co Donegal. Some years later she was the subject of a joint sea search by Irish and British rescue services, including the RNLI, off the north Donegal coast. She was eventually safely located. Later the *Ard Carna* was purchased by Paul Deasy, Union Hall. He fished for a number of years. Following her term at Union Hall, order of ownership is unclear but it appears that circa 1984 she was purchased by Patrick Friel, Ballywhoriskey, Fanad, Co Donegal. The final owner in Ireland was Dominic Orpen, Castletownbere. There may well have been another owner involved previous to Dominic, one whose identity evaded me. While still in excellent condition and a perfect example of a well maintained BIM 56-footer, she was sold out of fishing in 2011 to become a houseboat in England.

The *Ard Carna* at Castletownbere. Credit Oollit via *Trawler Photos*

7. *Ard Casta (D321)*

Builders: Crosshaven Boatyard, Co Cork.

Year of Issue: 1957.

Original Owner: Ernie O'Driscoll, Cape Clear, Co Cork.

First Homeport: Cape Clear, Co Cork.

Subsequent History: It's a history that can be summed up ever so briefly; a few months in the name of Ernie O'Driscoll previous to becoming the property of fellow Cape Clear man Joe Sheehan. When Joe stepped down, his sons Paudie and Thomas took over. The *Ard Casta* is a superbly maintained vessel that over the years has remained a permanent fixture in the Sheehan family. Sadly, the boat that I well remember landing large catches of mackerel at Baltimore in the late 1950s and early '60, now like many of her ilk, has an uncertain future in fishing. Yet another Code of Practice victim is the likely outcome!

The *Ard Casta* leaving Baltimore pier. Credit Michael Minihane.

8. *Ard Chluain* (D349)

Builders: BIM Boatyard Killybegs, Co Donegal.

Year of Issue: 1958.

Original Owner: Louis Graham.

First Homeport: Dingle, Co Kerry.

Subsequent History: The *Ard Chluain* was the fifth vessel built under the Gaeltacht Boat Scheme. There was however some delay between the times she was ready for sea and when she was actually issued. In subsequent years, circa 1972, the *Ard Chluain* moved to the Aran Islands on the west coast where Gregory Conneely became her second and only other owner. While out of fishing at time of writing she remained moored at Killeany Bay, Inis Mor, Aran Islands.

The *Ard Chluain* at Kilronan. Credit M.Conneely

9. Ard Chroine (D237)

Builders: BIM Boatyard Killybegs, Co Donegal.

Year of Issue: 1960.

Original Owner: Joe Boyle (Joe Joe Phil).

First Homeport: Burtonport, Co Donegal.

Subsequent History: The *Ard Chroine* didn't stray far from the Burtonport area. I'm told that Joe Boyle was still fishing her out of Burtonport in the winter of 1971/'72. Later she was sold to local man Pat O'Donnell, in whose ownership she is said have remained for around twenty years. She was still fishing in 1995. It would appear that tonnage assigned to her was later sold off. Last sighting was a Cleggan, Galway in 2006.

10. Ard Ciaran (D311)

Builders: John Tyrrell & Sons Ltd, Arklow, Co Wicklow.

Year of Issue: 1960.

Original owner: Oliver Tallon.

First Homeport: Clogherhead, Co Louth.

Subsequent History: Following her time at Clogherhead she was sold to John McClements, Portavogie. When re-registered B280, and re-named *Our Carole* she sold on to Willie Lennon, Donaghadee. In 2002 she was decommissioned and sold across the water where ownership appears under the names Bonusmix Ltd, St Annes, Lancs, and Bob McIllwrath, Fleetwood.

The *Ard Ciaran* - note the characteristic Tyrrell bow. Credit Jim McArdle.

11. Ard Colm (D37)

Builders: BIM Boatyard Mevagh, Co Donegal.

Year of Issue: 1959.

Original Owner: BIM (Training Boat) – Icelandic skipper.

First Homeport: Non permanent.

Subsequent History: Initially she was employed in an instructional capacity for fishermen. The venture is reported to have been particularly unsuccessful. Following that period the *Ard Colm*, in the first instance passed on to Gregory Conneely, Aran Islands who fished for BIM. In 1964 Gregory's brother, John, purchased her from BIM. Her next homeport was Greencastle, Co Donegal where she was owned by Brian Farren circa 1983. Following the period at Greencastle, Brian sold her to Denis Coll, Inisbofin, Co Donegal. She was later lost at sea, fortunately with no loss of life.

12. Ard Dallan (D240)

Builders: John Tyrrell & Sons Ltd, Arklow, Co Wicklow.

Year of Issue: 1960.

Original Owner: Joe McBride.

First Homeport: Burtonport.

Subsequent History: The Burtonport based *Ard Dallan* fished from her homeport throughout the 1960s and early '70s. Skippered during some of those years by Paddy Bonner, she is reported to have herring-paired very successfully with the *Ard Mhuire*. Circa 1975 the *Ard Dallan* was sold on to Denis Cavanagh, Greencastle, Co Donegal. Some years later she moved on to Portavogie where when owned by Angus Carson she was re-registered to B323. The names of Frank Zych, Ardglass, Co Down and that of Milligan& Sons, Ardglass have also been mentioned in the ownership stakes. When last sighted, circa 2002, the *Ard Dallan* was tied up at Annagasson, Co Louth.

The *Ard Dallan*. Credit James Murray, Grimsby.

13. Ard Eireann (D106)

Builders: BIM Boatyard Baltimore, Co Cork.

Year of Issue: 1964.

Original Owner: Paudie Curran.

First Homeport: Dingle, Co Kerry.

Subsequent History: Greencastle, Co Donegal became a second homeport for many BIM boats. The *Ard Eireann* didn't break the mould! This time it was John McClenaghan who assumed ownership in the first instance, before passing her on Jim Cavanagh, Carrowhugh, Greencastle. During Jim's ownership she was occasionally fished by Brian Farren. Having been re-engined and fitted with a new wheelhouse she moved to the south coast where she was initially the property of Patsy Cadogan, Bantry, Co Cork. Latterly, she was owned by Jeremiah O' Callaghan, Schull, Co Cork, who fished her up to recent times. Now out of fishing, the possibility of conversion to a houseboat has been reported.

The *Ard Eireann* at Schull - 2010. Credit Paddy Roche.

14. Ard Finnian (D402)

Builders: BIM Boatyard Killybegs, Co Donegal.

Year of Issue: 1962.

Original Owner: Paddy Sugrue.

First Homeport: Howth, Co Dublin.

Subsequent History: Circa 1973 the *Ard Finnian* made the short journey from Howth to Skerries where she became the property Seamus Corr. Seamus had the boat re-engined and fished her for a few years. He then sold her to Michael Collins, Kilkeel, Co Down. There she was re-registered N211. Adrian Graham, also of Kilkeel, later purchased her from Michael. She appears to have been decommissioned around 2002. No further information on her whereabouts.

The *Ard Finnian*. Credit James Murray, Grimsby.

15 Ard Fionnbarr (D370)

Builders: BIM Boatyard Mevagh, Co Donegal.

Year of Issue: 1961.

Original Owner: Michael Flannery.

First Homeport: Dingle, Co Kerry.

Subsequent History: If only the history of all boats was so simple. The *Ard Fionnbarr* moved from Michael Flannery to Paddy (Patie) Casey at Portmagee, Co Kerry, and that's where she has remained. The best news of all is that she is still fishing with Johnny Casey, brother of Patie, now skipper and owner. She recently passed the Code of Practice with flying colours - long may she last!

The *Ard Fionnbarr* towing with Johnny Casey standing at the winch. Credit Roland O'Shea.

16. Ard Gillen (D453)

Builders: BIM Boatyard Killybegs, Co Donegal.

Year of Issue: 1967.

Original Owner: Tom Ferguson.

First Homeport: Skerries, Co Dublin.

Subsequent History: The *Ard Gillen* was the first in a succession of boats owned by Tom Ferguson. When Tom took delivery of the newly built 70ft *Kenure*, the *Ard Gillen* remained in the Ferguson family and was fished, I believe, for some years by his brother Mick. Following the Ferguson's ownership she was sold to Peter Campbell, then a resident of Skerries. Peter is known to have fished her for a number of years, on the east coast initially, but on the west coast for the most part. Next in the ownership chain was another Skerries man Ivan Wilde, who in turn sold her to Brian Furlong, Kilmore Quay, Co Wexford. Following several years of fishing out of Kilmore Quay, circa 2004 Brian sold her to Tom Dempsey, Arklow, Co Wicklow. The Arklow man later sold her on. By then her days were numbered and it's doubtful if she put to sea again. At any rate she deteriorated while tied up at Arklow pier and was eventually broken up in 2011.

The *Ard Gillen* at Arklow – 2007. Credit Mark Archer

17. Ard Ide (D344)

Builders: BIM Boatyard Mevagh, Co Donegal.

Year of Issue: 1962.

Original Owner: John Brosnan.

First Homeport: Dingle, Co Kerry.

Subsequent History: The *Ard Ide* appears to have spent all of her comparatively short life in Dingle. Now, in an advanced state of dereliction her remains lay on a nearby strand.

The *Ard Ide* permanently beached near Dingle. Credit Dutch via *Trawler Photos*

18. Ard Macha (D207)

Builders: BIM Boatyard Killybegs, Co Donegal.

Year of Issue: 1956.

Original Owner: Joe McGinley.

First Homeport: Burtonport/Teelin, Co Donegal.

Subsequent History: While the *Ard Macha* mainly fished out of Burtonport, she was inextricably linked with the small Donegal Bay port of Teelin. In the 1970s the *Ard Macha* changed hands, resulting in ownership going to Denny McKennedy, Union Hall, Co Cork. Following a longish stay at Union Hall she was next to become the property of Paddy Rath, Clogherhead, Co Louth. Having served time there she was to return to her first homeport, Burtonport, and to the ownership of Neil Doherty. Circa 1999/2000 for some reason she underwent a registration change from the original D207 to D387.

The *Ard Macha* at Burtonport . Photographer unknown.

19. Ard Mhuire (D5)

Builders: BIM Boatyard Mevagh, Co Donegal.

Year of Issue: 1958.

Original Owner: Willie Joe McBride.

First Homeport: Burtonport.

Subsequent History: According to a BIM report, in the early 1960s the *Ard Mhuire* "was engaged for prolonged periods in experimental fishing and instruction." However, while in the ownership of Willie Joe McBride, she is reported to have herring paired very successfully with the *Ard Dallan* in the late 1960s and early 1970s. Willie Joe a native of Gweedore, Co Donegal sold her on to William Farran, Greencastle, Co Donegal. In the 1980s he her sold to Michael Doherty, Glengad, Co Donegal. Circa 1988 she became the property of her final owner, Seamus Corr, Skerries. Fifteen years later she ended her days at the east coast port.

The *Ard Mhuire* approaching Skerries . Credit John Kinsella.

20. Ard Mor (D277)

Builders: Crosshaven Boatyard, Co Cork.

Year of Issue: 1957.

Original Owner: Batt Whelan.

First Homeport: Helvick, Co Waterford.

Subsequent History: Batt sold the Ard Mor on to fellow Helvick man Mossie Kelly. The next owner was John Connolly, Clogherhead. From Clogherhead she moved to Ardglass, Co Down where she was owned by Frank Zych. The move which took place around 1976 necessitated a registration change to B117. However the *Ard Mor* did not end her days north of the border but returned south where she underwent a registration to DA7. In Arklow she became the property of Brian Dempsey. Having gone out of fishing in 2006 she spent a number of years tied up. I understand she was broken up at Arklow some years ago.

The *Ard Mor* at Arklow circa 2007. Credit John Wichett.

21. Ard Rathain (D262)

Builders: BIM Boatyard Mevagh, Co Donegal.

Year of Issue: 1956.

Original Owner: Paraic Willie McDonagh.

First Homeport: Kilronan, Aran Islands, Co Galway.

Subsequent History: Following Paraic Willie's ownership the *Ard Rathain* passed on to Kieran Gill, Inis Mor, Aran Islands. Somebody I spoke to remember her pair fishing out of Killybegs with Willie Hegarty's BIM 56- footer *Twilight Star*. Next in the ownership stakes, circa 1969, was Gregory Conneely, Inis Mor, Aran Islands, who had her re-engined and re-winched. Five or so years later he sold her on to Pat Harrington, Baltimore who fished quite a lot on the west coast. Circa 1979 Seamus Corr, Skerries purchased her from Pat. Seamus sold her on to Dick Deasy, Union Hall some years later. In time Dick sold her to the partnership of Charles Crozier and Charles McKee of Kilkeel when she was re-registered N143. No further information!

22. Ard Scia (D55)

Builders: BIM Boatyard Killybegs, Co Donegal.

Year of Issue: 1966.

Original Owner: Kieran Gill.

First Homeport: Kilronan, Aran Islands, Co Galway.

Subsequent History: Kieran fished the *Ard Scia* until his untimely death in 1992. In the 1970s she formed a very successful pairing partnership with Gregory Conneely's *Connacht Ranger*. Following Kieran's death the *Ard Scia* was sold to Aran Island's man Tommy Flaherty who fished her for a number of years. At the time of writing she was being dismantled at Rossaveal.

The *Ard Scia.* Credit Eugene McShane.

23. Connacht Ranger (G47)

Builders: BIM Boatyard Killybegs, Co Donegal.

Year of Issue: 1970.

Original Owner: Gregory Conneely.

First Homeport: Kilronan, Aran Islands, Co Galway.

Subsequent History: The *Connacht Ranger,* along with the *Ard Aengus,* shares the distinction of having one owner only. In both cases the owner was Gregory Conneely.

The *Connacht Ranger at* Kilronan. Credit M.Conneely

24. Coolan (D90)

Builders: BIM Boatyard, Killybegs, Co Donegal.

Year of Issue: 1960.

Original Owners: Patrick Griffin & Thomas Sheehy.

First Homeport: Dingle, Co Kerry.

Subsequent History: From the original owners the *Coolan* passed on to Thomas Sheehy's son, Patrick. She was next purchased by John Arthur, Kenmare. A couple of years later she was sold on to Frank Doogan, Kincasslagh. In the 1970s the *Coolan* was sold to Scotland where she had a name and registration change, respectively to *Janeeta* and INS195. No further information!

25. Favourite (SO351)

Builders: BIM Boatyard, Dingle, Co Kerry.

Year of Issue: 1971.

Original Owner: James (Mickey Mor) Gallagher.

First Homeport: Burtonport, Co Donegal.

Subsequent History: Last 56-footer built. The *Favourite* remained James' property for a number of years before passing on to Ronnie Gemmel, Burtonport. During Ronnie's ownership she was fished very successfully by Frankie Byrne, Burtonport. Then a wheelhouse fire resulted in her going back to BIM. Six to eight months later she was sold to a man who seemed to put a lot of boats through his hands, Thomas Wills, Ardglass. Circa 1971 her registration number changed to B311. From Ardglass she moved to Ballyglass, Co Mayo where she was owned by Pat Walker. That move led to a further registration change – WT194. A final ownership change took her to Jason and Stevie Moore, Killybegs. She was decommissioned in 2011. Rumours of conversion to a pleasure craft were in the air.

The *Favourite* at Killybegs -2009. Credit Paddy Roche.

26. Girl Eileen (D13)

Builders: BIM Boatyard Killybegs, Co Donegal.

Year of Issue: 1957.

Original Owner: Mossey Moore.

First Homeport: Killybegs, Co Donegal.

Subsequent History: Mossey sold the *Girl Eileen* to Donie Deasy, Union Hall. Donie fished her for several years before selling her to Hugh Coffey Portavogie, in 1979. While there re-registration to B313 took place. Remaining in Portavogie, she passed on to Robert Coffey circa 1989. In 1991/'92 she was sold on to John (Ivan) Adair also of Portavogie. In the mid-1990s ownership passed on to Ian Bailey, a marine engineer. He intended having her converted to a houseboat. She subsequently fell into dereliction near Derry.

27. Glendalough (D310)

Builders: John Tyrrell & Sons Ltd, Arklow, Co Wicklow.

Year of Issue: 1957.

Original Owner: Bill Cleary.

First Homeport: Arklow, Co Wicklow.

Subsequent History: The Glendalough was purchased from Bill Cleary by Willie Bates, Kilmore Quay in the mid-1960s. Willie sold her to John Power, Kilmore Quay in 1969. In the early 1970s she was sold on to Dick Deasy Union Hall. Dick in turn sold her to Keith McIlroy, Kilkeel, Co Down where a registration change to B289 took place. From Kilkeel the *Glendalough* found her way into Scottish ownership and was decommissioned when registered CN291 in 1993. As a footnote Billy Bates (son of Willie) reminded me that the Glendalough might be recalled for her part in the search for a crashed Aer Lingus plane off the Tuskar Rock in 1968.

The *Glendalough* off Arklow. Credit Liam Spacey.

28. Glenmalure (D147)

Builders: John Tyrrell & Sons Ltd, Arklow, Co Wicklow.

Year of Issue: 1957.

Original Owner: Jack Bermingham.

First Homeport: Arklow, Co Wicklow.

Subsequent History: Jack Bermingham sold the Glenmalure to Jimmy Bates, Kilmore Quay, around the mid-1960s. Sadly, with the loss of one life, she sank near Hook Head in 1969.

The *Glenmalure* at Arklow. Credit Liam Spacey.

29. Guiding Star (D2)

Builders: BIM Boatyard Dingle, Co Kerry.

Year of Issue: 1964.

Original Owner: Paddy Flannery.

First Homeport: Dingle, Co Kerry.

Subsequent History: Paddy Flannery sold the *Guiding Star* to Paddy Power, Kilmore Quay in the late 1960s. She fished out of Kilmore Quay for many years, laterally under the guidance of Paddy's son Pat. In the mid-1990s she was sold on to Derek Mc Guinness, Rush, Co Dublin. There have been unsubstantiated rumours of a later owner, but one way or another she finished her days in the waters close to Skerries.

The *Guiding Star* departing Rosslare Harbour – 1989. Photo credit Brian K. Cleere via Joe Teesdale

30. Morning Star (D28)

Builders: BIM Boatyard Killybegs, Co Donegal.

Year of Issue: 1964.

Original Owner: Joe Walsh.

First Homeport: Dingle, Co Kerry.

Subsequent History: It would appear that the *Morning Star* was sold on to her only other owner, Stephen Attley, Skerries. It was there she ended her days. I understand that she was skippered for many years while at Skerries by Georgie Corr.

31. Naomh Brendain (D79)

Builders: John Tyrrell & Sons Ltd, Arklow, Co Wicklow.

Year of Issue: 1959.

Original Owner: Joe 'Babs' Flaherty

First Homeport: Dingle, Co Kerry.

Subsequent History: Joe Flaherty sold the Naomh Brendain to Thomas Joyce, Currane, Achill Island. Thomas in turn sold her to Paddy Kilbane, Cloughmore, Achill Island. The time span of ownerships could not be ascertained. However, in 2002 she appeared as a houseboat in England. Later still, in 2010, renamed *Dreamwater* she was advertised for sale.

***The Naomh Brendain*. Photographer unknown**

32. Roving Swan (D64)

Builders: BIM Boatyard Killybegs, Co Donegal.

Year of Issue: 1959.

Original Owner: Patrick Sheehy.

First Homeport: Dingle, Co Kerry.

Subsequent History: Patrick sold the *Roving Swan* to fellow Dingle man Brendan O'Rourke. Having fished for an unknown number of years he sold her to Paddy Hogan, Kinsale. Three years or so later she became the property of Jerry O'Driscoll, Kinsale. In 1975, during her years at Kinsale, it seems that an application to have her name changed to *Angela's Bell* failed. Jerry O'Driscoll sold her on to Padraig McDonagh, Rosaveal. As to her movements, nothing further could be verified until 2010 when she turned up as houseboat owned by Scuba Cliffy at Fleetwood. Scuba had purchased her at Kilrush, Co Clare.

The *Roving Swan* at Fleetwood – Credit Norman Pascoe.

33. San Marten (D305)

Builders: BIM Boatyard Meevagh, Co Donegal.

Year of Issue: 1957.

Original Owner: George McCallig.

First Homeport: Killybegs, Co Donegal.

Subsequent History: George sold the San Marten to Danny Gallagher, St John's Point, Co Donegal. The next owner appears to be Peter McGuinness, Killybegs. Registered N218 in 1974 she was then owned by Thomas Curran, Kilkeel and fished latterly by Thomas' son Gerry. She was decommissioned at Kilkeel.

34. Sancta Lucia (D4)

Builders: John Tyrrell & Sons Ltd, Arklow, Co Wicklow.

Year of Issue: 1959.

Original Owner: Jimmy O'Sullivan.

First Homeport: Cahirciveen, Co Kerry.

Subsequent History: When still a new boat and fishing at Dunmore East, the *Sancta Lucia* drifted ashore while brailing herring with her partner, the Scotch boat *Kestrel.* The *Kestrel* was rendered a total loss. The *Sancta Lucia,* though very badly damaged was salvaged by Jim Doyle, Wexford. She was towed to Kilmore Quay where she was rebuilt on the pier. As far as can be ascertained she went back fishing in the early 1960s, skippered by Mark Bates and remained fishing out of Kilmore Quay until the mid-1970s. She was then sold on to Martin Guildea, Balbriggan. A few years, circa 1991 she was purchased by P. Geraghty also of Balbriggan. Nothing known of her from the mid-1990s onwards!

35. Saoirse (D346)

Builders: BIM Boatyard Meevagh, Co Donegal.

Year of Issue: 1957.

Original Owner: Pat Deasy.

First Homeport: Raheen/Union Hall, Co Cork.

Subsequent History: To quote Pat Deasy, "The Saoirse arrived at Raheen on Biddy's Day 1958." (Biddy's Day – St Brigid's Day is the 1st of February). She was to remain at Raheen, immaculately kept, (that's my own observation, not Pat's) until the mid-1990s. She was then sold to the Goggin family at Schull, Co Cork. In 2005 when owned by Michael O'Callaghan, Schull, she sank at sea as result of a fire outbreak.

36. St Bernadette (D57)

Builders: BIM Boatyard Meevagh, Co Donegal.

Year of Issue: 1958.

Original Owner: Gerry O'Shea.

First Homeport: Castletownbere.

Subsequent History: Gerry came to own the *St Bernadette* mainly because the *Ros Beara*, the boat he was fishing at time, was damaged in an accidental collision while fishing at Dunmore East. While the damage was being sorted he was without a boat and knowing there was an unallocated 56-footer at Meevagh, suggested to BIM that he would take her. However in a matter of years Gerry moved to bigger boats and it was while the *St Bernadette* was tied up at Howth that his brother Teddy took her over and in time moved to Killybegs. When Teddy got his own boat, the *Charlotte Chambers*, the *St Bernadette* was sold to Mick Cavanagh, Arklow. Next owner was Union Hall man Denny Deasy. Denny in turn later sold her to Brendan Walsh, Rosslare. From Rosslare she moved up the Irish Sea and found a new homeport on the Co Down coast when owned by a member of the Chambers family. Then bearing the registration number B274, she passed on the William George Graham, Kilkeel, who had her name changed to *Autumn Sun*. By that time the much travelled boat was getting tired and seems to have ended her days in Kilkeel.

37. St Catherine (D299)

Builders: BIM Boatyard Killybegs, Co Donegal.

Year of Issue: 1957.

Original Owner: Seamus Murrin.

First Homeport: Killybegs, Co Donegal.

Subsequent History: The *St Catherine* was one of those boats to find a very comfortable second home port and remained there. In 1977 Seamus Murrin sold her to Michael O'Gorman, Achill Island. At time of writing the family owned boat is in excellent condition and happily fishing, now under the guiding hand of Michael's son, James.

The *St Catherine* at Achill Island. Credit Brendan Minish

38. St Joseph (D111)

Builders: BIM Boatyard Killybegs, Co Donegal.

Year of Issue: 1960.

Original Owner: Paddy O'Regan.

First Homeport: Schull, Co Cork.

Subsequent History: Paddy O'Regan sold the *St Joseph* to Charles Kelly, Greencastle. Best information after that is that Barney Curran, Kilkeel became her next owner. While she still had her original registration number in 1978, twenty years later it had changed to N263. She appears to have been decommissioned in the mid-2000s.

The *St Joseph*. Photo via Greencastle Museum

39. Twilight Star (D412)

Builders: BIM Boatyard Killybegs, Co Donegal.

Year of Issue: 1958.

Original Owner: Brian Gallagher.

First Homeport: Killybegs, Co Donegal.

Subsequent History: Another one of those much travelled boats! First it was a change of ownership in Killybegs from Brian Gallagher to Willie Hegarty. Willie later sold her on to Don McKenna, Howth. Christopher O'Rourke who fished her is said to have been a part owner. From Howth she moved to Portavogie where Johnny Adair became her new owner. Associated with that move was a registration change to B141. It was unusual for BIM 56-footers that went to Co Down ports to return south. However, the *Twilight Star* did just that when purchased by Dick Deasy, Union Hall. During Dick's term of ownership her cabin was moved from forehead to aft. When purchased by Cara Rawden, the restless boat was to find yet another homeport at Greencastle where she was fished by Brian Farren. Following her spell at Greencastle she made a final move to Owen Brannigan at Skerries. There she ended her days. Of interest is that her registration number changed from the original D412 to B141 (Portavogie) back to D412 (Union Hall) to SO198 (probably at Greencastle).

The *Twilight Star* fishing off Skerries. Credit John Kinsella

Part III

Maritime Experiences

Gerry Doyle

Renowned Kilkeel fisherman Gerry Doyle – 2011. Credit P. Nolan.

Gerry Doyle, renowned Kilkeel fisherman of yesteryear, and presently an active octogenarian, first opened his eyes at Kilmorney Cottage on the shores of Kilkeel harbour. The harbour of that era is virtually unrecognisable when compared to the modern complex. However, the location of Kilmorney Cottage can be accurately pinpointed because it was situated on the site of present day RNLI Lifeboat Station. Young Gerry could scarcely have been born closer to the sea and throughout his lifetime he was seldom to be found far from it. I was, he said, "Totally absorbed with fishing since I was a child."

When he left school his mother's wish that he should attend Atlantic College, Dublin to undertake a radio operator's course foundered when it was discovered that he would have to wait for a number of years before the required admission age was attained.

A Step Up

Instead, at the age of fifteen, and one of a family of six children, three boys and three girls, Gerry joined the crew of the *Esse Cully (B116),* a boat skippered by his father. That was in 1944! Memories of that period include herring drift netting during the summer and Danish seine net 'fly-dragging' for whiting during the winter. As was the custom at the time boats were painted in springtime by their crews in advance of summer herring drift netting. A first season working out of Howth was Gerry's initiation to the world of commercial fishing. He remembers that his father fished the *Esse Cully* very successfully.

As time went on, Barney McComish, owner of the *Esse Cully*, became interested in buying the *Eventide (B386),* a younger boat, fitted with a 5L3 Gardner 85h.p. Furthermore he offered Gerry's father a full partnership; a great opportunity but one requiring a £700 deposit - a lot of money! A sum which Mr Doyle felt was well out of his reach. Yet, when he somewhat forlornly relayed the opportunity to his wife Annie, a dressmaker, she fondly assured him that *they would raise the money*. It was a tender moment all those years ago in the lives of Gerry's parents that brought a tear to his eye as he related the incident to me. "Great memories", he remarked. The *Eventide* was indeed purchased as planned!

In the year or so that followed, Gerry fished on the *Eventide* with his father. Then, along came a major blow to the family! While Gerry was still in his eighteenth year his father died at the age of forty-two. The man who had been an exemplary parent and husband, sailed on steamboats, unfailingly sent home the bulk of his wages, built a new house that became the family home, and successfully skippered fishing boats, departed this life at a very early age. Gerry was left to pick up the pieces and in doing so took over as skipper of the *Eventide*. His brother John had gone through secondary school education with a view to becoming a chemist. Once again the lure of the sea won out when he joined the crew of the *Eventide*. Gerry recalls, "John and I ended up fishing. We went to Dunmore herring drifting in 1955. We both loved fishing and we did very well. Those who know would agree that I was among the top skippers at the port here, on and off, for four or five years."

While the *Eventide* remained under the Doyle stewardship, Gerry purchased the Buckie based 65ft, *Coreopsis (BCK172),* and younger brother John took command of the *Eventide*. The *Coreopsis,* a boat of 18ft beam and almost 7ft of draught was Devon built, probably towards the end of World War 11. She was a standard British Admiralty motor fishing vessel that had been re-engined and re-wired six months previous to purchase. A well found boat for her age! Herring fishing with her during the winter of 1957/'58, for most part involved the use of a seine nets and coil, or even a half-coil-aside. It was, Gerry said, "A case of dropping the net and virtually plucking it out of the water as quickly as possible." While the *Coreopsis* set a record by landing £2,000 worth of herring at Milford Haven during one week in the late 1950s, her owner described her as 'a stupid boat to manoeuvre'. That observation, if I understand it correctly, came from the reluctance of some boats to respond quickly to the wheel/rudder. It was a factor that made them somewhat unsuitable for herring seining. I was disappointed at Gerry's description of the boat I remember being as prominent as he was during Dunmore East herring fishing seasons of the late 1950s. However, I know what he meant!

The *Coreopsis* laden with herring entering Lerwick Harbour. Credit Shetland Museum via Gerry Doyle.

The boat will be well remembered for one particular incident in February 1958. Based on Gerry's recall I will attempt to give an abridged version of the happening. He describes the account as, "a cautionary tale for small boat seamen." It began in Milford Haven with what he says was, "A little bad judgement, which an older more cautious skipper might not have made."

During the Dunmore East herring season of 1957/'58, higher prices paid at Milford Haven and Holyhead led to the *Coreopsis*, and indeed other boats, to occasionally land catches at those ports. Following one such landing at Milford Haven in February 1958

A Step Up

Gerry and his crew spent a stormy night moored off shore. By morning the wind had eased and the crew were anxious to get underway. Gerry was aware the storm had not passed but rather that they were sitting in the eye. He believes that while a more cautious skipper would have contented himself and stayed put, somewhat influenced by a young and enthusiastic crew *he* made the decision to head off. The hope was that they would make the crossing to Dunmore East before the wind got up again. He accepts full responsibility for the decision taken, explaining that he was wise enough to make up his own mind. The crew were Brendan Mc Dowell, Annalong; James Donnan, Kilkeel; Robbie Rodgers, Longstone; Hugh James Rodgers, Longstone; and Bill Hudson, ex Fleetwood, then living in Kilkeel. The *Coreopsis* motored out past St Ann's Head into a huge south-easterly swell, but with no wind. On they went past the Smalls as fast as the 114hp Gardner could drive the boat. As signs of a 'south-easter' became imminent, his mind shot back over many years and acted on advice given to him by his father when little more than a boy – 'keep windward, and keep plenty of water under you'. By the time they had the Tuskar bearing north it was blowing hard. Obviously they were well past the point where return to Milford Haven or Fishguard was not an option. The decision Gerry had to make was whether to run for Rosslare (2hrs) or head for Dunmore (3.5 hrs). He decided to go for the devil he knew best and headed for Dunmore. As Gerry put it, "By the time we had the Coningbeg Ship abeam there was a lot of wind and a very big sea running. It was also dark and raining, and in those days we had no radar in our type of boats." He went on to say, "But we did have DECCA, and by that time I was anxious enough to be keeping a good eye on that invaluable piece of equipment. My intention was to keep a good offing until we opened the estuary up to Waterford. I don't believe anyone aboard was worried about the boat. I certainly wasn't! She was like a little duck, not a bother to her. The odd time I pulled her up head-on and slowed down the engine for a breaking sea but it was prudence not worry that prompted the action. On one occasion there was a sharp crack and a board was blown out of the lee bulwark. That happened when she was on top of a big sea, and halfway into her roll to weather. The wind and sea during that part of the run was about two points abaft our port beam. I was worried about damage to the DECCA aerial as I intended to run in past the Hook and on into Dunmore East on purple lane 56."

The skipper and crew of the *Coreopsis* had reached a point where a review of their circumstances became necessary. A certain amount of anxiety was generated by the fact that Gerry had been in touch with other skippers on the R.T. and all were warning him to take care, 'as there was some very bad weather about'. Jimmy Thomson, skipper of the *Kincora (INS 100),* one of these men, Gerry said, "You took heed of," had run up past Duncannon and commented that that he had had 'all the weather he wanted'. He went on to advise Gerry not to chance the Bar as it was getting worse by the minute. Decision time dawned for Gerry! The options were stand off for the night or continue on to Dunmore! He and Annalong man, Brendan McDowell, were in the wheelhouse. Brendan concurred with Gerry, in the prevailing conditions and the likelihood of even worsening weather ahead, the better option was to attempt the 'run into Dunmore'. The crew were made aware of the decision. Everything possible was checked out, with emphasis on the state of the engine room. Instructions were issued to close everything up, and on no account to open the galley door. In the wheelhouse, Brendan was on engine control standby, and Gerry was on the wheel. He squared the boat on the purple lane with the Hook flashing on the starboard bow. All seemed to be going well! With Dunmore dead ahead they were running in nicely on lane 56. Then without warning Gerry was taken by surprise when the sea took complete charge! Brendan instantly pulled back the throttle and moved the gears to neutral. It took a moment for them to realise what exactly was happening. This is how Gerry describes the period that followed, "The side windows of the wheelhouse were submerged in white water but the front windows were clear. The boat was shuddering in a way a small plane shudders just before takeoff. We were actually surfing on a big sea. I think Brendan realised at the same time as I did what was happening. Out in the galley the rest of the crew were also wondering what was going on. The aft end of the casing was submerged in green water that wanted in. One of the men, James Donnan of Kilkeel, was down in the cabin but there was enough water getting through the cabin skylight to persuade him to evacuate. Soon, all hands bar Gerry and Brendan McDowell, crowded the galley where the water was ankle high. Their nerve held, they sat tight, and had the presence of mind to close the hatch so that water didn't have free access into the cabin. James Donnan's wisecracks helped! He excelled himself in the midst of the ordeal and had the others laughing at his antics. It says a lot for the crew that they didn't crowd into the wheelhouse; none of us had previously experienced the likes of what was happening that night."

What Gerry and his crew didn't know then was that their nightmare was far from over. The saga as told by Gerry continues, "An exchange of terse messages took place between myself and Hubert Griffiths, skipper of the *Feaco*, a Milford Haven vessel. Hubert's boat was anchored at Passage East. I knew he was on standby, as indeed were a dozen others willing us to safety, because I had spoken to him ten minutes earlier. My latest message was, Hubert, we might be in trouble, alert the Dunmore East Lifeboat. I learned later that coxswain Stephen Whittle and his crew were already on alert and had actually overheard my message to Hubert. Shortly afterwards a sea ran over us and cleared the decks of everything that was not bolted down. The boat kept going straight as an arrow until the sea passed her. During the brief respite that followed we went on deck to ascertain that the propeller was clear before engaging the clutch. A cursory glance enlightened us to the fact us that, nets, ropes, timber, the loose poop deck over the steering gear, and every bit of loose dunnage had all been swept overboard. Back in the wheel house, we were about to engage the clutch when a shout was heard from aft. One of the crew had spotted that the anchor chain was overboard and that the end of it was well and truly fast on the little beam that supported the poop deck. Towing the chain may well have saved us from broaching on that sea. You wouldn't expect a ¾ inch chain to wash overboard! We managed to hand haul the chain and closed up the casing."

Back in the wheelhouse again, Gerry checked his bearings and was amazed to find the distance the boat had travelled, largely out of control, on that particular sea. They were then east-north-east of Dunmore with the cliffs of Credan Head on their lee. The estimated distance to Dunmore was about three miles. Taking up Gerry's account, he said, "Talk about running the gauntlet, there were big breakers roaring everywhere, but we pressed on. We were port side to the weather and away on the port bow I could see a breaker roaring down on us. Proximity of the shore ruled out surfing! I hauled her up to come head on but the closer the sea came, the bigger and steeper it got. I reckoned that if I drove into it the casing would be ripped from the deck and that all hands would go overboard with it. Every instinct told me that the boat couldn't survive end-on. It was then that the sea lore gathered by long teenage ears came to mind – *when the chips are down, leave your boat broadside*. I didn't quite leave her broadside; I left her two points into the wind, and waited. It was the longest minute I have ever experienced! First of all we were on an even keel and the wind had momentarily stopped whistling. Gently the boat started rolling to starboard and I remember saying to Brendan, she's going to be alright, she's rolling away from it! That's what I was hoping for! The alternatives, which I kept to myself, were either to be smashed up or rolled over! Neither happened, like a game little animal she put her head four points to starboard and took off like a surfing expert along the base of the sea. She was lying over on her starboard side. Only the buoyancy and perhaps the planing lift of the wheelhouse were preventing her from completely capsizing. On she went and shuddered her way from under the big comber. Once clear, she rolled back to her portside and away she went like the thoroughbred she was! I can easily get emotional when I think of that game little boat. Five minutes later we slipped in past the pier light at Dunmore. All mooring ropes and fenders had been washed overboard, so we dodged about the harbour until the crew got the anchor shackled up and dropped. When Bill Hudson (the man who did most of the cooking) went to make tea he eventually found the kettle in the top bunk. The conclusion to be drawn is that the starboard roll when we surfed on the second sea was well over 90 degrees, probably 110 degrees."

Gerry honestly believes that their safe arrival in Dunmore East was down to the help of six guardian angels and five good seamen. He just happened to be the one in the driver's seat.

Today Gerry reflects on the generosity and solidarity among fisher-folk and their supporting community ashore. Thanks to those attributes the *Coreopsis* was back fishing one week later. New fishing gear was pressed on them by nearly every fisherman in the fleet, and repairs free of charge were carried out post haste to the casing, poop deck and pound boards by the shipwrights of Waterford Harbour Board.

All's well that ends well, but there is a lesson to be learnt! Gerry hopes that in the reading of his experience, young men in small boats will think twice before putting to sea in dubious weather conditions.

Gerry fished the *Coreopsis* for about four years. As time passed he concentrated more on trawling and reckons that he was up there with the most successful fishermen on the Irish coast - "I made a great name for myself as a seaman," he said.

He recalls that in the mid to late 1950s the importance of trawl types used in Scandinavian countries came to the fore. It became clear that the catching potential of those trawls was much greater than those hitherto used on the Irish coast. The *Resolution*, a boat owned and skippered by Dan Griffin, Schull, was out-fishing all other boats for some considerable time before it became common knowledge that he was using a particular type of Danish trawl. Victor Chambers, Annalong later benefited greatly when he began to use a similar net. It was Gerry said, "Almost two years before we got one. A great period of fishing followed for us! It was one of those periods that come the way of all fishermen. It is when you feel that you can't go wrong. You get on a roll, confidence is high, and no matter where you drop a net it comes up full."

It was during that period Gerry had DECCA installed in the *Coreopsis*. It came about as follows, "Annalong man Victor Chambers, who was certainly the main skipper in these parts at the time, considered me as an up and coming fisherman. We frequently compared notes and at one point concluded that to fish further afield was the way forward. With that in mind we considered DECCA to be essential. I took the bull by the horns and became the first skipper in Ireland to order it, knowing that there was a minimum six month waiting list. It was quite a step at a time when a crew member's weekly wage averaged around £5, and the cost of hiring (units were not for sale) this new piece of instrumentation was £15 per week. (i.e. equivalent to about three shares). Still, I had confidence in the investment! I was happy that it was the right thing to do! That I was not actually the first to have DECCA installed came about because a new boat being built for Jack Chambers was nearing completion, and on request I gave up my place in the queue so that Jack's boat came out of the yard with the unit fitted. I settled for second place!"

The *Croidte an Duin*. Courtesy Gerry Doyle.

In 1959 Gerry felt the time was right to move up to a bigger boat. His brother John took over the *Coreopsis*, and he purchased the oak-on-oak 86ft *Madame Prunier (LT343)* for £6,000. Built in 1948 at Brooke Marine Ltd, Lowestoft she was Kilkeel's biggest boat of the day. He changed her name to *Croidte an Duin*. The plan was that the two boats, *Coreopsis* and *Croidte an Duin*, would work to pay off *Croidte an Duin*. Previous to Gerry's ownership the boat had been engaged in line fishing and had never been used as a trawler. Briefly he was tempted to continue line fishing but changed his mind and had her rigged out for trawling. A few years later fairly major work carried out on the *Croidte an Duin*, included re-engining and a substantial change in wheelhouse configuration. The original HRL Crossley 265 h.p. reversible 2-stroke engine was replaced by a 240h.p. Kelvin - "A big, big mistake," said Gerry. "There was not a thing wrong with the engine, it seldom gave trouble, but the horse power was too low. The boat towed well enough in calm weather conditions but otherwise not so. There was no problem herring fishing but white fish trawling could be very problematic." Casting his mind back to the days of the *Croidte an Duin*, he recalled having 90 tonnes of herring aboard her when 'pair-fishing' with Davey Wilson's *Shemariah* in 1967. It was the largest landing of herring from a single boat at that time in Kilkeel. He recalled too that he was always able to get the best of crews, and spoke of his long association with John McDowell, a man who fished a lifetime with him. John he said was, "A great man, a great teacher! He put a lot of young fellows aspiring to be fishermen through his hands. They came to us on a half-share basis and stayed as such until they had learned to mend (nets). Some of them of course moved on to other boats, but those to whom they went were confident that the men they were getting had learned their trade well as half-share men with Gerry Doyle and John McDowell." Thinking aloud he went on to say, "I never drank alcohol myself, took the pledge at fourteen years of age. I had to mind my money from a very early age and seldom had money in my pocket."

In the early 1970s circumstances prompted Gerry to invest in another boat. His brother John bought the *Grainula* in Sweden and suggested to Gerry that he should go for a similar boat that was also for sale in Sweden. Gerry went along with the suggestion, he purchased the 80ft *Clipper* (D330) and John McDowell took over as skipper of the *Croidte an Duin*. The newly acquired big boats were the first fishing vessels in Ireland to be fitted with net winches, a feature which facilitated larger mesh nets and made hauling less arduous.

A few lucrative seasons herring fishing out of Galway followed the arrival of the *Clipper*; so much so, that she 'cleared' herself in two seasons. At that time Gerry became involved with other skippers in attempts to form a co-operative at Galway. For what seems like a variety of reasons the attempts were largely thwarted. While some progress was made, and on paper a co-op was formed, the outcome appears to be far from satisfactory. It was an outcome that one way and another generated a degree of ill feeling amongst members. Apparently it didn't work out great by any means. They did however fight a court case against the Galway Harbour Authorities, a body intent on banning fishing vessels from the harbour. While they didn't win the case, the judge instructed both parties to go off and sort out their differences, making it clear that he didn't want see them back in front of him again. However, Sean McBride, their legal representative, regarded the outcome as a victory – fishing boats continued to use the harbour.

All was going well with Gerry in the world of fishing, that is, until one day in March 1977 when fishing off Erris Head, Co Mayo. In his own words he says, "The experiences of that day and the period that followed are unlikely to recede far from my memory." Here I've attempted to summarise the sequence of events as told by Gerry! There was good trawling ground north and east of Erris Head at an area known as the 'Stags'. On that particular day a cold easterly wind was backing southerly when they had hauled and shot again during the small hours of the morning. With the recent catch safely iced away in the fish room, Gerry went to bed for awhile. Three hours later crewman Paul O'Reilly called him. He believed the weather was deteriorating and wanted the skipper to check it out. Gerry went to the wheelhouse to find a full gale blowing and decided to haul the trawl. He called two other boats in the vicinity, John McDowell in the *Croidte an Duin* and Killybegs man Noel McGing in the *Olgarry*. Both were underway for Killybegs having hauled a couple of hours earlier. The *Clipper* was a side-winder. When they came broadside to haul, such was the rolling of the boat that it made working on deck very uncomfortable indeed. They were shortened up to the last mark when Gerry noticed that one of the young crewmen, Michael Green, had the rather precarious job of unhooking a messenger (a length of nylon rope) off the after trawl door. He became concerned because at the time Michael was not very experienced and feared somewhat for his safety. As such, Gerry who was in the wheelhouse indicated to Michael that he would go out and unhook the messenger himself. That he did as soon the trawl door came up to the gallows. While it was possible to reach the messenger from the deck it was easier to do so if one stood on the gunwale/rail. Using the gallows leg to steady himself he unhooked the nylon rope and passed it to the next man who hooked it to the net winch. A smooth enough operation that when carried out gave him a moment to look around! What he saw bearing down on the boat was a 'bad sea'. With no time for him to get off the rail he held on tight to the gallows and screamed a warning, *'big sea, lookout, big sea'*, though he doubts if anyone heard the actual words. However, in spite of the howling wind and a roaring comber bearing down on them they got the message. Normally he would have been in the wheelhouse and given the warning sooner, because he says, "It's very much part of a fishing skipper's job to watch out for danger of any sort."

However, when the sea hit the quarter took the brunt of it. Yet, it rolled aboard solid from the quarter to the whaleback. Gerry was still standing on the rail and the men on deck were up to their thighs in water. When a heavy sea like that hits a boat it shunts her violently and Gerry became aware of the steel warp attached to the trawl door screaming out through the gallows block a foot from his face. He believes it certainly would have parted had the winch brake been screwed tighter. The winch paid out enough warp to leave the trawl door dangling between the rail and the water. Engulfed by incoming water Gerry held on to the gallows in order to prevent himself being smashed against the wheelhouse. While he succeeded in that part, pressure due to the mass and volume of water returning overboard caused him to lose his hold. He was washed overboard and he found himself in the water close to the boat and looking up at an eight foot steel trawl door! He realised immediately that the door would hit the water when the boat rolled back to starboard. He was facing the boat and instinctively tried to get away from where he thought the door would come down. In that he succeeded, the door hit water less than a foot from his shoulder rather than on the top of his head. Instinctively he grabbed the door bracket with both hands and scrambled on to it before it started to rise again. There is invariably a smooth stretch of water behind big rogue seas, so that gave him an interval in which to climb aboard.

Problematic though it was, with the help of Paul O'Reilly, he eventually did manage to get back on deck.

Perhaps he says, "My Guardian Angel intervened when I was in the water because I had considered swimming for the headline of the net. I figured that the crew could haul me aboard with the net winch. Just as well I didn't go for that option because the impact of the sea had swept the boat away from the net so violently that a hydraulic pipe burst and put the winch out of action."

Back on deck he went to help repair the burst hydraulic pipe but was so wet and cold that he began to shake uncontrollably. He was not wearing oilskins because normally he wouldn't be on deck during hauling. He made for the heat of the engine room, stripped off and lay across the engine until he stopped shaking. A change of clothes and further heat from the engine seemed to bring his body temperature under control. He went up to the wheelhouse and manoeuvred the boat while the net was being hauled. As he squared away for Killybegs everything was normal but soon he began to feel nauseous. He called the *Croidte an Duin* on the R.T. and told John Mc Dowell, who was already aware of the earlier incident, that he wasn't feeling well. Paul O'Reilly would take charge of the wheel while he went to bed. Gerry asked John to watch out for them on the radar and keep in touch with Paul. They were six hours out from Killybegs. Gerry believed he would be fine in an hour or so. Noel in the *Olgarry* was also in touch. Both he and John slowed down their boats until the *Clipper* caught up a bit and they had good radar echo.

Half-an-hour passed! Gerry heavily wrapped up in his bunk still felt cold and began to feel unwell with chest, neck and arm pains. He became very worried! Thoughts of people he had known with similar symptoms entered his mind. One suffered a heart attack, the other was found dead in his bunk. With those thoughts in mind he got out of the bunk and proceeded to the wheelhouse. He told Paul he thought he was having a heart attack and needed help. Back in the cabin again he told the boys what he wanted – "all the blankets and sleeping bags available, wrap me up as warm as possible and help wedge me under the table." It was low down in the boat and the table legs prevented him from moving when the boat took a heavy roll. He didn't want to be left alone and had young Robert Kearney stay with him. Robert, a mere teenager, understandable became a little fidgety as time passed. The prospect of sitting with a man who may well be dying was far from desirable. As time passed he warmed up and in order to help set Robert at ease, sent him to make a mug of hot, sweet tea. As he lay there, Gerry felt sorry for himself, crying a little, while thoughts of his wife Josie and their children were foremost in his mind. He prayed that God would take care of them and lamented that Niall, their youngest child, would have no memory of him. While making the cup of tea helped to put Robert at ease, it helped Gerry also, because he fell asleep and when he woke up the pain was gone.

A Step Up

Less than six hours or so later John McDowell talked a competent but inexperienced Paul O'Reilly past Rotten Island and into Killybegs harbour. John then transferred to the *Clipper*, leaving his son William in charge of the *Croidte an Duin*. With the minimum of fuss the *Clipper* was berthed and before Gerry knew what was happening two paramedics arrived at the top of the cabin companionway. While the paramedics discussed how best to get him up out of the cabin, he climbed the ladder unaided. Once on the pier he was ushered to a waiting ambulance that had previously been arranged by Noel McGing. Comfortable and heavily sedated, the journey to Letterkenny Hospital seemed to pass quickly. Later he woke up in an intensive care ward where over the next four weeks the consultant and staff at the hospital stabilised and looked after him. It was quickly established that he had suffered a serious heart attack. Thus began a long emotional and thoughtful period in his life!

Following the traumatic incident off Erris Head it took six months before Gerry was able to walk the furlong from his home to the shore bank, and a further six months before he was permitted to drive a motor car. During that period he came to understand the need for religion, something he believes is inherent in all of us.

John McDowell who had sailed as mate with Gerry for almost thirty years, and a very special friend, took charge of the *Clipper*. John's son, William, was appointed skipper of the *Croidte an Duin*. At least Gerry had no worries on that score; the boats were in good hands. However, his wife Josie had plenty to worry about, not least the fact that she had four young children, one an infant, to look after. Throughout the four weeks Gerry lay in intensive care at Letterkenny Hospital, Josie made the three hour journey back and forth from Kilkeel in her 'little VW Beetle'. Gerry says, "It wasn't always easy but with the help of God and a few good friends, she managed." He went on to say, "What we didn't know then was that her pilgrimages were far from over."

Once back at home Gerry felt pretty sure that all would soon be well with his health, and that he would be back fishing in a few weeks. He complied religiously with doctor's orders. Yet, his GP Dr Carroll saw reason to put him under the care of a specialist, Dr Scott, at the Belfast City Hospital. Gerry continued to believe that there was nothing to be over perturbed about – a matter of weeks would see him back to full health. He would be back to work in no time. Well, he did get back to work, but not in a matter weeks. It was in fact four years later!

During that four year period all had not gone well for the Kilkeel man where 'material matters' were concerned. John McDowell had become unhappy with the controllable pitch propeller fitted on the *Clipper*. This resulted in the *Clipper* being tied up and John returning to the *Criodte an Duin*. That led to a decision being taken to put the *Clipper* up for sale. There was a glut of boats on the market. As a result one year later she remained unsold. Then what appeared to be a way out came when a young Danish fisherman based at Grimsby showed an interest in taking her over to fish in the North

Sea. Gerry, having experienced so many good Danish fishermen over the years, was easily persuaded to let the young man have the boat. It was something he was to regret, and summed up the decision in the following words, "A financial disaster is the short story of that venture. When I did manage to extricate the boat from Grimsby she had a damaged engine." Basically, the engine needed to be replaced. An insurance claim made was met with a great deal of tardiness on the part of the company. A new engine was to cost £35,000 but the company were only prepared to pay £22,000. He says, "With hindsight I should have pursued the claim more vigorously by getting a lawyer to deal with the insurance company. I had been paying premiums without making a claim for many, many years and now the company baulked when I needed them. The problem is that hindsight is not available when it is most useful and somehow life has to go on."

The outcome of the fiasco was that the *Clipper* lay idle for a few years. It was during those years that the Government decided to 'clean up' the fishing register. The *Clipper* became a casualty, ruled redundant tonnage on the grounds that she had been idle for so long. Her licence was revoked! As a consequence when they worked out quota allocations she was excluded. The sad part of it was that over the lay-up period Gerry had made stringent efforts to get the boat back fishing. Had he not been let down by the seller of a good second hand engine the *Clipper* would indeed have been back at sea. Instead, a fine eighty-foot Swedish built boat, oak on oak, became a liability at the stroke of a civil service pen and had to be disposed of. Gerry argued the case for a re-issue of the licence to no avail. As he says, "The cookie had crumbled and civil servants can be very objective."

Not yet ready to throw in the towel, Gerry invested the insurance money from the *Clipper* in yet another boat. In the early 1980s he bought the *Ocean Trust (B267)*. With the same propulsion unit as the *Clipper* and a more modern winch, the *Ocean Trust*, although Norwegian built was a Swedish type boat.

The *Ocean Trust*. Courtesy Gerry Doyle.

Gerry went back to fishing in his latest acquisition. Alas, it was short lived! In 1985 heart trouble again reared its head, eventually necessitating artery by-pass surgery. Recuperation took the best part of two years. A further blow came Gerry's way around the time of the bye-pass procedure when his lifetime friend and colleague, indeed oft times his right-hand man, John McDowell died.

Eventually Gerry returned to fishing the *Ocean Trust*. The *Croidte an Duin* had been disposed of by then. Terms such as, 'log book and quota' were becoming common place in commercial fishing vocabulary. Unfortunately the 'control years' on which the quotas were based coincided with the lay off from fishing following Gerry's bye-pass and John McDowell's death. Consequently records showed that Gerry's boat/boats did little fishing during the 'control years.' As a result when the Producers Organisation portioned the quota among the various boats he came out very badly – went from having a lot of quota at one time to very little. When decommissioning came Gerry took it on the *Ocean Trust*.

Gerry's interest in boats and fishing was later to be revived when his son Niall decided that he wanted to try his hand. The *Green Pastures*, a Norwegian built vessel, powered by a Caterpillar 805 b.h.p. engine, became the property of the Doyle family. Purchased without licence or quota, both had to be acquired. The boat is described by Gerry as, "The best I ever had."

The *Green Pastures* at Kilkeel. Courtesy Gerry Doyle.

Niall took over the boat and was Gerry said, "Working away very steadily, going ahead at least, and not going down anyway." Then as fishing restrictions and increasing overheads came along it became more difficult to earn a livelihood. Slowly pelagic fishing began to die a death in Kilkeel. Father and son, with father as deck hand, fished the boat for awhile. They did very well in the month of January one year, landing about £45,000 worth of fish. The work, according to Gerry, "Was tough enough in terms of hours put in, but where fishing was concerned it was relatively easy. When trawling for cod in the wintertime, to haul twice a day is sufficient. You could even tow for twenty-four hours. Cod are strong fish. They would still be alive and in good shape. The thing is if you hauled after four hours you may not get any fish." The logic here, as I understand it, is that if the fish swim long enough in front of the trawl mouth they will eventually suffer fatigue and drop back into the cod end.

In the longer term try as they might, scarcity of fish, the high cost of fuel, and the introduction of a raft of new restrictions on fishing made it impossible to earn a livelihood. There was only one way to go – decommission. The *Green Pastures* was scrapped at Fleetwood in 2003. By then Gerry was well into his seventies. His long and distinguished career in fishing finally came to an end. A lifetime in fishing indeed!

When I asked Gerry if all his ambitions and expectations in the world of fishing had been fulfilled, without hesitation he replied, "I would have liked to have got a newly built boat." That he never had a brand new boat was certainly not for want of trying.

A Step Up

By 1963 when he put in an application for a new purse seiner, he had already been unsuccessful with five previous similar applications. Amazingly, the 'powers that be' turned him down on each occasion. Undaunted, he tried again in 1965, that time his application was for a 'tank boat'. Once again those hard working civil servants found reason not to support his claim. It does make one wonder!

He recalls a somewhat bizarre situation arising when he showed an interest the not so new BIM (An Bord Iascaigh Mhara) owned *Loch Lein.* The *Loch Lein* was one of three 95ft offshore fishing vessels purchased in Germany by BIM around 1952. They were named *Loch Lein, Loch Laoi* and *Loch Lorgan.* Over the eight or so years in the ownership of BIM their fishing and profitability performance was abysmal, showing a loss year in, year out. Finally, in 1960 the Board decided that further losses could not be justified and decided to put the boats up for sale. That is where Gerry came in. He journeyed to Dublin to discuss the possibility of acquiring the *Loch Lein.* During the course of the discussion/interview he happened to refer to the Republic as The Free State. Such a reference would have been commonly used by Northern Ireland people in years gone by. That's the title they grew up with and it was spoken in the absence of derogatory overtones of any kind. However, Gerry reckons that's the rock he perished on. The gentleman across the tabled reminded him in no uncertain terms that the correct name of the country is the Republic of Ireland. From that moment onwards the chances of the Kilkeel man acquiring the *Loch Lein* took a dramatic downward turn. She was not to sail north!

While in Gerry's company I met up with Howard Forsythe, another legendry Kilkeel fisherman. The three of us paid a visit to the Nautilus Centre. When told by a pair of sea aristocrats that the Centre was a must see place, I had no doubt but it was just that. The highly impressive, modern Centre which opened in 1997 overlooks the picturesque harbour and houses the *Mourne Maritime Visitor Centre, Kilkeel Tourist Information Centre* and *Mourne Seafood Cookery School.* My interest focused mainly on the Maritime Centre and particularly a multimedia system which at the touch of a computer screen gives extensive information on local fishing and maritime heritage. Connor Keenan, Maritime Project Officer at The Centre, received us warmly, and for my benefit demonstrated the wonders of touch screen technology. It would be amiss not to mention that the Maritime Centre, and indeed The Nautilus Centre as a whole houses many other attractions, even craft activities for kids who visit. It is indeed a worthwhile stop-off for visitors to the area.

At the Centre the three of us sat for a while and chatted! The manner in which the two men conversed, and the banter that took place between them left one in no doubt as to the friendship and camaraderie that existed over their many years at sea. Howard joked about Gerry's mishap when, as was a sixteen year old fishing with his father, he fell overboard. The story went, "We were fishing nearby and the next thing I saw him swimming in the water. He had come on deck and somehow fallen overboard! We were getting ready to pick him up when his father spotted him. Ah, sure he was only a chicken then." The two men laughed heartily!

Howard's presence reminded Gerry to tell what he described as a horror sea passage. It took place around 1956/'57 when they were both respectively running herring from the Dunmore East fishing grounds to Holyhead in the *Coreopsis and Bonny Lass (*Howards boat at the time). Gerry headed away north before Howard. Shortly afterwards he noticed that the boat was behaving a little oddly and on investigation found that she was taking in water – a leaked had developed around a deck ring. Water coming in over the boat was finding its way down inside her. He couldn't pump her out because she was full of herring. What was he to do? He couldn't continue driving on hard into the weather. She would fill up! He decided to carry on but slowed down and pulled in close to shore where the sea was calmer. He continued up along the Irish coast and, as he put it, "When almost level with Howth ran across to Holyhead."

Meanwhile Howard had long since arrived in Holyhead. He had no inkling of his fellow traveller's problem. To his surprise, and concern, Gerry wasn't there. Howard said, "He had left before me, and he had a bigger and better boat than I. I asked the guy on the quay if the *Coreopsis* had come in. No, she had not he answered. I went up to the headland to see if there was any trace of her coming and boy was I relieved when I spotted the *Coreopsis* making her way in. I noticed that she was low in the water. Gerry related the whole story to me when he arrived in. I rigged up a pump and sorted him out."

So ended my get-together with Gerry and Howard!

Sean O'Driscoll

Sean and Kathleen O'Driscoll at Dunmore East – 2010. Credit P. Nolan.

My earliest recollection of Sean O'Driscoll is that of a teenager fishing out of Baltimore during a spring mackerel fishing season. It must have been in 1953 or '54. The Cape Clear Island native fished on the *Carbery Lass*, a boat built through a Congested District Board loan in the early 1900s, and one of the few Cape Clear fishing vessels to survive the 1930s depression. Many of her contemporaries were sold on while others rotted at Tra Chiarain on the Island. However, that was all a long time ago, and now fifty-six or fifty-seven years since my initial recollection of Sean, I find myself slowly driving along a country road in the vicinity of Killea Church on the outskirts of Dunmore East, Co Waterford. I look at house after house, none seemed to fit the description I had been given, but I carry on. Just as I'm beginning to doubt whether I'm on the right road or not, I spot this tanned, fit looking gentleman mowing a lawn. Instantly recognisable after all the years is Sean!

A Step Up

Having warmly welcomed me, he remarked, with an intimation of 'how he has changed' in his voice, "I expected you to look as you did in Baltimore all those years ago." In fairness he attempted to cheer me up a bit by adding, "It was a long time ago and we've all changed a lot." Yes I thought, but obviously some have changed more than others! I had been told that Sean frequents the gym and that he strikes a golf ball as good as most in Dunmore East. Perhaps that accounts for the difference! Outside his home we stood and admired the wonderful southerly vista overlooking the sun drenched sparkling sea all the way to the unmistakable land mark that is Hook Head.

The purpose of my visit was to learn something of Sean's long and varied fishing career, and perhaps his views on an industry to which he has devoted a lifetime. First, along with his wife Kathleen, a most amicable Co Waterford woman with scarcely a trace of that county's fairly distinctive accent, we chatted awhile. I asked Sean how he originally became involved with fishing. His answer, "It was inevitable, it was in the blood, and anyway for the most part that's what young men on the island did in those days." It was an answer that made sense when one considers that over the years not only did Sean become a high profile fisherman but so did his brothers Donnchadh and Pat.

Following a season or two on the *Carbery Lass*, Sean joined the crew of the now late Peter Downey's newly built BIM 50-footer, *Ros Droichead*. That he recalls as being 'a big shift' in 1955. Two years 'ringing' in the *Ros Droichead* were followed by a season mackerel fishing in the *Eventide*, a smart 47ft boat, that had recently been purchased by the Cape Clear Cadogan brothers, Pat and John; otherwise known as Pat Bill and John Bill. The next step in Sean's career progression took place when he joined the crew of the 55ft *Radiance*, a boat skippered by his brother Donnchadh.

Sean's most outstanding memory of fishing on the *Radiance* was that of herring purse seining at Dunmore East. It was he said, "A very effective way of working and thanks to the help given by the skipper and crew of the St Ives boat, *Sweet Promise*, through time we got good at it." He went on to say that in a matter of a few years the advent of seining and mid-water trawling put paid to purse seining. He recalled that while Cornish men helped the *Radiance* crew to hone the art of purse seining, a similar situation arose when seining was first introduced to these shores. This time it was Scotchmen who first came to help out the skippers and crews of the brand new, identical, and classy Tyrrell built boats, *Glenmalure* and *Glendalough.* Thinking aloud, as it were, Sean added, "I believe the first boats to mid-water trawl for herring in Dunmore were skippered by Brian Crummy, Dunmore East and Kevin Mallon, Arklow."

By the early 1960s, at around twenty years of age Sean became skipper of the 60ft *St Gerard,* a boat in which he had an ownership interest. In the mid-1960s she underwent fairly extensive renovation which included the fitting of a new Rolls Royce engine. He recalls the years that followed as being exhilarating times in fishing at Dunmore East. There was he said, "A real buzz about the place, exciting times indeed. The money for herring was good. We did very well in the *St Gerard* mid-watering with the Scotch boat, *Unity*, skippered by Harvey Sloan, Girvan. There were up to ninety boats in the harbour in the wintertime."

The *Crimson Dawn*. Photographer unknown.

Following his term in the *St Gerard*, Sean bought the 75ft *Primula* from Mick Doyle, Killybegs. She was he said, "Getting old at the time but a fine boat fitted with 152hp Gardner engine. We did well enough with her. After a few years I sold her and had the brand new *Crimson Dawn (W119)* built."

Unfortunately, the Campbeltown built *Crimson Dawn*, launched on a day of high wind and lashing rain in the spring of 1976, proved to be an extremely problematic vessel! Reflective words said it all, "She could have been so good, a fine boat, but with engine problems right from the very start she was a nightmare." As a consequence Sean parted company with her. Shortly afterwards he joined the crew of Mick Doyle's super trawler, *Paula (D165)*, at Killybegs, and fished on her until 1986.

It was a move that he regards as being up there with the very best he made in his fishing career. His words, "It was a fabulous job, no worthwhile work at all in it, and fantastic money. Mick was ashore, the boat was being fished by John Poole, Wexford. We were mackerel fishing; pairing with Teddy O'Shea's *Sheanne*. Catches of up to 300 tons in one tow were not uncommon. When Mick Doyle got the 120ft beamer, *Dolores*, a lovely boat, I moved on to her as skipper. Perhaps I should have stayed on the *Paula,* the fishing she was engaged in got even better in subsequent years. Having said that, we did very well beaming on the *Dolores* in Morecombe Bay! That was especially true of the early years we fished there. Sole, were very plentiful. It was a time when the North Sea was virtually devoid of that species. Accordingly there was huge money for catches landed from Morecombe Bay. Gerry O'Shea (Castletownbere & Howth) was also beaming there in the *Marie Jacob*; he knew the ground a bit better than we did. He once grossed £62,000 for a six day trip, a massive amount of money then. I loved beaming and stayed at it until the *Dolores* was sold in 1991."

Not one to hang around, Sean temporarily fished out of Newlyn, Cornwall. Next move was to skipper the Clogherhead boat, *Newgrange*, then owned by Seamus Connolly. It was a stepping stone to his skippering another of Seamus Connolly's boats, the *Linda C*. "A fine boat," he says, "I fished on her in the North Sea for three years. I really loved it! We landed regularly at the Danish port of Thyboron. To visit home we travelled back to Holland and flew from Amsterdam to Dublin. It was great! But all good things come to an end! For one reason and another I decided to return home. I suppose the time had come to wind down a little."

Not yet ready to take retirement though, back home Sean fished the Duncannon boat *Renegade* for Kevin Downes, for awhile. Later he moved on to Johnny Keating's (Kilmore Quay) *Briget Carmel*, a boat he fished from 1997 until 2001. His swan song in what was undoubtedly a glittering fishing career was played out during the years he skippered the Kilmore Quay, Flatherty owned *Quay Fisher.* The curtain fell on that final act in 2008. What a fishing career indeed! It all began from humble beginnings in the 1950s when as little more than a boy he joined the crew of Joe O'Driscoll's *Carbery Lass* to try his hand at drift netting during a spring mackerel fishing season at Baltimore.

It was obvious that for the most part Sean greatly enjoyed his days as a fisherman. Ability to adjust either when he chose to do so, or when circumstances demanded, is testimony to his versatility. He was never going to be out of a job! Now in retirement I asked how he views the fishing industry. What are his observations? He begins by telling me, "I feel very sad when I go down around the harbour in Dunmore. I just can't help thinking back over the years and find it hard come to terms with the transformation that has taken place." He believes that nationwide a disastrous situation has developed through lack of will and understanding on the part of successive governments to further the cause of fishermen. He recalled hearing of an incident purported to have taken place in Dail Eireann in 1935; a particular T.D. put forward a proposal that as priority urgent steps should be taken to set about establishing a long term plan for the development of the fishing industry in this country. The proposal was apparently met with derision and treated as a matter of amusement by at least some of those present. While current members of 'the house' may not show such obvious disdain, the same mentality would appear to prevail. The fishing industry appears to be regarded as a joke, or at least not a significant national asset! Sean believes that government personnel now appear to take pleasure in enforcing to the letter of the law, obstructive bureaucratic dictates handed down from a European Commission of which friends of Irish fishermen are few and far between.

Sean believes that the apathy shown towards commercial fishing by our landlubber leaders over many years has left the majority of people in our small country ignorant of the sea and what goes on in and around it. In contrast he said, "When we used to land in Denmark, I remember meeting Scandinavians, many of them had no connection with the sea, they were inland people, but they had a great knowledge of it. They knew about fishing and what it entails! In Ireland, like our politicians, many people living less than a mile from the sea are not remotely interested in what is going on. It's a pity!"

On the question of crippling bureaucracy that has crept in to make life virtually intolerable for fishermen, Sean cites a few examples, "When I started fishing you bought a boat, registered her and you went fishing. You never saw an official again! As far as I was concerned that was freedom! Now you can't look around but there is somebody there telling you what you are doing wrong, or that you must do this or that. I just couldn't hack it. It's all wrong. It's the reason I retired from fishing when I did." He went on to talk about how the bureaucratic system operates here compared to other E.U. countries, and quoted the following as an example, "A Kilmore Quay man bought a 36ft boat with tonnage at Stornoway in the Outer Hebrides. Because the solicitor acting for him was based in Northern Ireland the boat was registered there. When paperwork regarding the tonnage transfer was drawn up the owner was required to sign his name in three places. Having done so he was told that he was free to take the boat, and that he could begin fishing immediately if he chose to do so. Now, had the owner elected to have his business conducted in the Republic of Ireland, crazy officialdom would have seen him waiting for six months, or maybe up to a year, before getting clearance to go fishing."

A Step Up

Some of what goes on would be laughable if the implications weren't so serious for those directly involved or indeed for the industry as a whole. In recent times another gem regarding tonnage emerged. This is how Sean explained the scenario, "It used to be that when a boat was sold within the country there was no bother getting the boat's tonnage transferred to the new owner. Not anymore! The seller of a boat is now obliged to hand the tonnage back to the Department and the buyer has to apply for it. By implication there is no guarantee that the new owner will get the tonnage, so he might end up with a boat but no tonnage. It's nonsense, it doesn't happen in any other country. It seems to be that things are constantly being made more difficult for fishermen in this country."

Like other people I meet on my travels, Sean is of the opinion that with the best will in the world there is no such thing as an influential fisheries minister, and no matter how the title is parcelled up, (currently Minister of Agriculture, Fisheries and Food), the individual carrying that label is merely a mouthpiece. He or she is limited to delivering what is permissible by departmental civil servants, possibly even an assistant secretary. With a smile on his face Sean recalled an incident that took place in Howth many years ago. This is how it went, "I had the *Crimson Dawn* at the time and we used to land our fish around 5am in time for the Dublin market. One particular morning we were the only boat there and I was approached by a man who asked if I would like to speak with the Minister for Fisheries. At first I was a little reluctant, in fact I declined. Ah, but the minister would like to talk to you, I was told! I agreed, so over he came, shook hands and said hello. No sooner had he uttered the greeting than his escort approached and brusquely addressing the minister advised that it was time to move on. The minister mildly protested, saying I have only just met this man. The escort's response was to persist with ushering the minister towards a waiting car. I thought to myself I have as much authority in the Fisheries Department as he has."

Before taking my leave we talked about members of his family who were also heavily involved with fishing. I recall that his father, Denis, fished in two boats that I knew of, the *Inane* owned by Cape Clear man Pat Bill Cadogan and the afore mentioned *Radiance*. Sean recalled that the island men in those days loved the spring mackerel fishing at Baltimore. He said that, "While it was hard graft, the money made was good enough. It came at the end of the winter and was almost regarded as a holiday, or at least a diversion from the island way of life." Later on came Sean's brothers Pat and Donnchadh. During the 1970s and '80 Pat owned and fished the 75-ft *Green Eagle* and the 100-ft *Golden Dawn*. Donncha, who was widely regarded as one of life's gentlemen and a fisherman supreme skippered a series of what were big boats at the time! Included were the *Radiance*, *Castlebay* and *Golden Harvest*, boats in which he had partnership interests. In 1975 he acquired his own boat, the brand new 70ft, Baltimore built *Northern Dawn*. When he sold on the *Northern Dawn* seven years later, he replaced her with another new boat, the 75ft Dingle built, *Resplendent*. As the

1980s wore on, illness forced Donnchadh into early retirement. Sadly, at the age of 58, this previously fit man, a teetotaller and non-smoker departed this life – Ar dheis De go raibh a anam!

As Sean and Kathleen bade me adios on an ever so lovely August evening, I had the distinct feeling of having spent the afternoon with old friends!

Kieran Cotter

Kieran Cotter - Volunteer coxswain of the Baltimore all-weather Tamar Class RNLI Lifeboat, *Alan Massey*. Credit P.Nolan

On my travels around West Cork I met up with Kieran Cotter at Baltimore. Kieran is a man steeped in all that's maritime related. While not quite of the age group I usually concentrate on, his family background and association with the sea and seafaring make up for his lesser birthday count. Seldom have I met a man with such a keen insight, thorough understanding and deep interest in all that's positive where sea related activities on coastal villages are concerned.

Kieran, one of a family of five, four brothers and one sister, was born on Cape Clear in 1955. His father was part owner of a few fishing boats and also ran a business on the Island. From an early age the young Cotter boy was very much aware of fishing activities carried out in and around Cape Clear – spring mackerel drift netting and summer lobster fishing being foremost. Amongst his earliest recollections of boats in which his father had shares were the *Radiance, St Gerard and Castle Bay*. While the

A Step Up

Radiance, a boat of around 55ft, did engage in mackerel drift netting out of Baltimore in the 1950s, the larger *St Gerard* (60ft),and the *Castle Bay* (70ft), concentrated on trawling. The latter boats seldom came home to Cape Clear or Baltimore, working instead out of ports such as Dunmore East and Howth.

In 1970 the Cotter family moved from Cape Clear and settled in Baltimore. While his secondary school education was still ongoing Kieran spent summer holidays salmon fishing in a 26ft family owned boat, the *North Bay*. At that particular time, 1970/71, he says, "Salmon drift netting took off big-time here. In a matter of a few years there were about fifteen half-deckers working out of Baltimore. The first year we were involved was 1971, a season that proved very successful. At around the same time a Frenchman introduced shrimp pots locally. All of a sudden there were forty or fifty small boats shrimp fishing in and around Baltimore Harbour, Roaringwater Bay and along the coast towards Schull. Shrimp fishing on a commercial scale had not been carried out around here previously, though it is true that BIM had conducted experimental tests which had proved positive. 'Shrimping' developed quickly and is still ongoing. The main difference between the present day way of working and that of the early 1970s is that similar sized boats fish up to eight hundred pots, more likely to be between four to six hundred, as opposed to the twenty to forty then fished." It was interesting to hear that in the very first season shrimp processing (cooking) was carried out in part of a long defunct school building in the village, before shipping to France.

In September 1973 Kieran joined the state owned deep-sea shipping company, Irish Shipping, as a cadet. Irish Shipping was formed during World War 11 for the purpose of supplying the country's needs. In post war years the company continued to operate as a commercial strategic reserve until 1984, when for one reason and another it was forced into liquidation. Kieran's first year with the company was spent high-sea globetrotting, with New Orleans, several passages through the Panama Canal, a Pacific Ocean crossing to Japan, and a west coast of Canada trip among the highlights. Next on the agenda was a period at a Nautical College in Plymouth. That completed, he returned to summer salmon seasons in Baltimore, and a few winters herring fishing and trawling out of Dunmore East. Vessels he fished on included the 80ft *Johnny Ruth*, a boat built at the BIM Yard, Baltimore in 1975, the *Golden Harvest,* and Sean O'Driscoll's, Campbeltown built *Crimson Dawn.*

Kieran made what can possibly be described as a life defining decision in 1975 when he became a volunteer crew member of the Baltimore offshore RNLI Lifeboat. It was the beginning of a lifelong association that would see him appointed volunteer coxswain in 1989, a position he has since held. Initially, fishing commitments regularly took him away from home and as such was only available for occasional callouts. That was to change! In 1977 at the prompting of his father he purchased a commercial business overlooking the pier and harbour in the heart of Baltimore village. From then on he became a regular volunteer crew member – more on that later! Following a major constructional makeover the newly purchased business began trading mainly as a grocery mini supermarket with an additional business where fishing tackle could be purchased. In the years that followed, with Kieran by then married to Brigid, he went on to trade significantly in the purchase and sale of commercial fishing nets, the procuring of which took him to countries such as Denmark, Japan and Taiwan. The business developed further to trade in hardware and fuels. It continues to offer a comprehensive service for fishing vessels and other craft visiting the port of Baltimore.

The Mariners Friend **(47-029), a Tyne Class Lifeboat (as the *Hilda Jarrett* (47–024)), being launched from the RNLI boathouse at Baltimore. Credit-late P.Hickey.**

Kieran recalls, “I became very much involved with the lifeboat from 1982 onwards. Around that time I was appointed second coxswain, and in the summer of 1989 when the incumbent coxswain Christy Collins retired, I was appointed volunteer coxswain of the all-weather Tyne class *Hilda Jarrett*, a position I still hold. Having been granted a further five year extension as coxswain I'm very much looking forward to the arrival of a new Tamar class boat in early 2012. The *Hilda Jarrett* has served the station well but the fact is that after twenty odd years of service she is classed as obsolete.”

A Step Up

When I asked Kieran if he had any outstanding memories of lifeboat callouts, he responded by saying, “Over the years we have had lots of cases, some with sad outcomes, some with joyous outcomes, and some unusual cases.” One that immediately came to mind was the disappearance of the 65ft fishing vessel, *St Gervase*, with the loss of all hands. He recalls the sequence of events as follows, “We received a phone call around 3.00am on November 23rd 2000 to the effect that EPIRB tracer signals were picked up from the *St Gervase*, a vessel with a crew of four that had left Castletownbere over two hours previously. It was reported to be on its way to fishing grounds off the Seven Heads. As a result of unsuccessful efforts to contact the vessel, the rescue services in the area were being tasked. We launched the lifeboat and based on information received proceeded in the direction of the Fastnet area. From drawing a line on a chart between Castletownbere and the fishing ground we reckoned that was the furthest the *St Gervase* could have got in the given time interval. There was no sighting in that area so we made our way towards the Mizen. Just as dawn was breaking we noticed an oil slick on the water and floating nearby was a lifebelt with a flashing light. There was no trace of the boat or the crewmen! The stark reality for the lifeboat crew on that bleak November morning was that the search was over! We contacted Valencia Radio relayed the sad news and requested that divers be sent to the scene. All search units were promptly directed to the area. A large swell made it unsuitable for an immediate dive. However, the following morning divers located the wreck and also the body of a crew member. Having collided with the north side of Mizen, the *St Gervase* had foundered.”

In contrast, about fifteen years prior to the *St Gervase* tragedy, a late night callout to a 50ft motor yacht that had foundered near Mizen Head resulted in a happy outcome. As the lifeboat reached the vicinity crew members spotted four people in a dingy. The occupants of the dingy, who were at the time unknown to the lifeboat crew, were taken on board. Kieran takes up the story, “Twenty minutes or so on the way back to Baltimore we were all sitting in the aft cabin when suddenly one of the more observant lifeboat crewmen leaned forward and congratulated a member of the rescued party on the celebration of his 60th birthday. The penny dropped! Most of us present then recognised the man as none other than current Taoiseach, C.J. Haughey, known to all and sundry as Charlie Haughey!” It would also appear that the identity of those rescued may not have been immediately know ashore, as when the name of the sunken vessel, *Terema 11,* was reported by the lifeboat, a message came back unusually asking to have it spelled out ; recognition of name identified the motor yacht as that of the Taoiseach. Later she was discovered sunk at a depth of 15meters just beneath the Mizen Head Lighthouse. Two contrasting outcomes from misadventures in the same sea area; all hands lost in the *St Gervase* incident, all saved in the case of the *Terema 11*!

A Step Up

When I asked about unusual incidents, Kieran replied, "I suppose the one-and-a-half tons of cocaine had to be the most unusual." The reference was to a call out in July 2007 when the Baltimore Lifeboat and its crew were at the centre of news story regarding a major drug smuggling operation that went badly wrong. This is how he remembers the incident, "A call came through that someone was missing at sea for four or five hours. Now, the sad fact is that when someone is missing at sea for so long and *not wearing a life jacket* the call becomes less urgent. We launched, proceeded to the vicinity and searched for a couple of hours. Throughout we had been listening to radio conversations between a searching Irish Coast Guard helicopter and the Castletownbere Lifeboat to the effect that a man had earlier been rescued from the sea. In the course of their conversations mention was made of packages floating in the water. We continued to search on the south side of the Mizen and soon saw bales floating in the water. The helicopter was having difficulty in picking them up and requested that we give them a hand. We took fifty-five bales aboard and landed them at Baltimore. While we suspected drugs, we thought perhaps cannabis. It never crossed our minds that it might be cocaine. The picked-up bales were right in on the shore." Yes, I remarked to Kieran, at the time I saw television pictures of the Baltimore Lifeboat lifting bales and though that boat is ever so close to the rocky shore. To which the coxswain he replied, "Those lifeboats are very easy to manoeuvre and anyway we're trained for working along the shore. There are occasions when it can be necessary to carry out a rescue from turbulent surf close to the shore."

Whetted by the accounts I had heard, I asked Kieran if he could recall the callout that involved the most hours away from base. He thought briefly before saying, "It was probably the Spanish trawler in 1991." He recalled the mission as follows, "We were called out on a November night in 1991 to a Spanish trawler in difficulty twenty miles west of the Fastnet. As we proceeded a very high swell and strong winds made the going difficult. Eventually we reached the disabled vessel. It took an hour for the crew of the 120ft Spanish trawler, *Japonica*, to secure a tow line. That done we headed for Castletownbere with the boat on tow. About four miles south-west of the entrance, in a huge swell and very strong south-westerly wind the three inch, braided nylon hawser gave way. This time the tow was re-establish much more quickly because the crew of the trawler could see that they were heading at high speed towards the shore. The tow continued in very difficult weather conditions into Bantry Bay where the trawler dropped anchor. For reasons best known to them, those in charge on the *Japonica* did not want to dock at Castletownbere. We continued on into Bantry, had breakfast, and set out to return home. By then the *Japonica* was being towed away by another Spanish trawler. On passage out towards Sheep's Head the lifeboat's engine developed filter problems which necessitated us diverting to Castletownbere. Additionally one of our crew who had fallen as the boat came off a big sea and suffered a head injury needed attention. No sooner had we arrived in Castletownbere, or maybe even before hand, than we received a call to the effect that a vessel was in difficulty thirty-five miles off. One hour later with a new filter fitted we headed out and towed the disabled yacht, *Atlantis Adventure*, into Castletownbere. By the time we arrived back in Baltimore we had been twenty-six hours on duty."

While Kieran did not tell me as much, I later learned that he was awarded the *RNLI Bronze Medal,* and that his crew received *Framed Letters of Thanks* for the rescue of fifteen people on the *Japonica* that night. I further learned that for that same service Kieran received the *Maud Smith Award* for the bravest act of lifesaving in 1991.

As we sat in the first floor sitting room of the Cotter family home, Kieran continued to recall his experiences. Our vantage point afforded a magnificent panoramic seaward view that not only encompassed Baltimore's so picturesque harbour, but also to the west, as far as the eye could see, many of the aptly named 'Carbery's Hundred Isles'. He began by describing what a typical summertime callout for a lifeboat might be, "A person or persons in a small boat, sailing or otherwise, has/have become fatigued because, for example, an engine has broken down or problems have arisen with sails. Very often there may be only a couple on the boat; frequently a husband and wife. They become overwhelmed by a particular situation. Usually it's something fairly simple that goes wrong initially; then other factors such sea sickness and fatigue conspires to accelerate panic levels. In those cases when we reach the casualty we launch our dingy, put two of our crew onboard who check on the welfare of the stricken vessel's crew before setting up a tow line." He went on to say, "A callout that was common in the past but one that is not received any more is that of a boat, usually a fishing vessel, with a flooded engine room. Many of those boats were ex-French, not in great condition and without bilge alarms. Very often the fact that a boat was taking in water only came to the attention of the crew when flooding caused the engine to stop. In those cases we went out, put a pump aboard the casualty, pumped the water out and towed the boat to a port. Such callouts have disappeared over the past ten or so years because boats now-a-days have bilge alarms fitted, and thanks to obligatory surveys, vessels are in better condition. Fishermen are now working in a much safer environment."

Yet, there are times when unforeseen circumstances can still cause problems. He recalled one particular callout when the lifeboat went to the assistance of a well maintained Union Hall fishing boat, the *Floralie*. She was taking in water and reached the stage where her engine room was beginning to flood. The usual lifeboat procedure of pumping out and towing the vessel ashore was carried out. All the common sources of leaks were checked out but nothing was found to be amiss. The boat was later dry-docked at an Oldcourt Boatyard, near Baltimore, for closer inspection. As a result it was revealed that a bolt or piece cylindrical metal had fallen into the bilges, where over a long period of time it continued to roll to and fro as prompted by the motion of the boat. The rolling action, which had probably gone on for years, had worn part of what was originally a three inch plank to virtually zero thickness; so thin that water easily found its way through. A most unusual scenario indeed!

Kieran places enormous importance on any aid that helps prevent loss of life at sea. Thankfully he says, "The regular wearing of lifejackets began in the 1990s. Most now wear them but some still don't. It's so important that all do so! It's vital whether on commercial or pleasure vessels. When on deck for whatever reason the wearing of a lifejacket is a must! Should an individual fall overboard wearing a jacket, his or her chances of survival are increased by ninety-five per cent. The importance of buying into any device that helps to save lives at sea should indeed be a priority wherever and whenever boating is taking place. Yet, to the dismay of many, including Kieran, the appropriate government department of this country has shown considerable 'coolness' to a Man Over-Board Guardian System (MOB) development by the RNLI. Without going into details of how the system operates, suffice to say, this 21st century aid to lifesaving at sea has the capability of automatically and immediately alerting RNLI headquarters at Poole, Dorset, to a man overboard situation. Accompanying the alert are details such as the time and position of the mishap. In the first instance, personnel at Poole attempt to make contact with the casualty. If that fails contact is made with the lifeboat station closest to the emergency and the lifeboat goes out to investigate. Kieran pointed out that, "All emergency services, including lifeboats, are today capable of a very swift response. However, in preference to moving towards implementing this vital lifesaving device, marine surveyors at the Department of Transport want all emergency alerts routed to the Coast Guard, and will not accept them via RNLI operational control in the UK." He goes on to emphasise, "The Coast Guard is absolutely excellent. Eighty per cent of our callouts and information come through Coast Guard personnel. However, if for whatever reason the casualty cannot make contact with the Coast Guard, then that particular route to the lifeboat breaks down. That's when the direct link becomes invaluable. Arguably lives would have been saved in at least three small boat tragedies on the Irish coast in recent years had the MOB Guardian System been an element of the craft's safety devices.

On the topic of fast response to callouts, I enquired as to what the routine time interval between alert and launch might be. First Kieran explained that at all stations the RNLI appointed LOM (Lifeboat Operations Manager) has sole discretion regarding the lifeboat launch – he decides whether a launch is to take place or not. If he deems it necessary, then he alerts the crew and informs the coxswain and mechanic of the relevant details. In mayday situations the crew could possibly be alerted directly by the Coast Guard, but in all other cases the Coast Guard telephones the LOM and requests a launch. Where the crew are concerned the process of alerting them has been greatly streamlined over the years. The booming sounds of maroons (rockets) are no longer heard, and the telephone call to individuals has also been dispensed with. Crew members are now alerted via bleeper only. As to the time interval between bleeper being activated and actual launch, in the case of the Baltimore all-weather lifeboat, Kieran says, "From activation of bleeper to launch takes six to seven minutes, provided one is up and dressed, otherwise it may take up to five minutes longer." A further speeding up of response will be achieved when the faster state-of-the-art Tamar class vessel comes on station.

It also has to be remembered that stationed at Baltimore since 2008 is an Atlantic 75 inshore lifeboat, *Bessie*. *Bessie* is capable of speeds up to 32 knots, can operate in conditions up to near gale Force 7 and carries a crew of three. She provides a rapid response to inshore emergencies.

When reflecting on the histories of lifeboats stationed at Baltimore an interesting point emerged. The station boat during the period 1984/'87 was the Oakley class *Charles Henry*. She put to sea in atrocious conditions on a November night in 1986 when steering failure caused the 170,000 ton bulk carrier, *Kowloon Bridge*, to collide with the Stags Rocks and sink with its cargo of iron ore. Fortunately the crew were safely airlifted. However, when coming off a massive sea during the callout the *Charles Henry* took a severe knock. Later, back at the station signs of paintwork cracking were noticed on the hull. Detailed inspection revealed that structural damage had taken place. She was immediately replaced by another boat at the station.

We began to talk in more general terms about Baltimore and its seafaring future. Substantial redevelopment work, carried out at both piers in recent years, leads Kieran to believe that a bright future lies ahead for the harbour area. Fortunes of the fishing industry at the port have fluctuated greatly over the past century, and continue to do so. In the early 1990s eleven trawlers, averaging 60ft in length, were at one time based there. By the early 2000s the number had decreased to eight. In more recent years, decommissioning and general ageing of vessels have accounted for a further decrease. That is not to say that trawlers from other ports do not land fish at Baltimore. As a registered port for the landing of herring and mackerel, Baltimore is occasionally used by pelagic boats from Castletownbere, Dingle and Galway. An important incentive for such landings is that Ilen Seafoods, a fish processing plant that handles large quantities of fish, particularly of the pelagic variety in the wintertime, is located adjacent to the village. Kieran feels that the improved pier, harbour and landing facilities give reason for future optimism where the local fishing industry is concerned.

The newly extended north pier at Baltimore – July 2012. Credit P.Nolan.

The fact that Baltimore pier and splendid harbour has more than one string to its bow is immediately evident to even the casual visitor, particularly so during the summer months. While fishing may well be traditionally associated with the port, the comings and goings of ferry boats to the offshore islands of Sherkin and Cape Clear, and the variety of sea associated leisure activities makes for considerable bustle at the seafront. Kieran says the ferries are very important. Not only are they used by natives and their friends, but the lure of the islands attracts large numbers of people who pass through the village on their way to visit and vice versa. Commodities and vehicles are also transported to the islands from Baltimore. Recent redevelopments to the ferry pier (old pier), and the building of a new slipway located away from the inner pier area which facilitates roll-on/roll-off (ro-ro) vessels have brought immense improvements to the services offered. Of interest to boat owners, pleasure or otherwise, is that when the slipway in not in use by ferry vessels, it is available to all users. Sounds like the perfect place for day trippers to launch or haul up a boat. In recent times the main pier has undergone a major refurbishment, part of which included having its original length of approximately 76m extended to 140m.

Ongoing sailing tuition at Baltimore. Credit P.Nolan.

Kieran waxed lyrical on the topic of leisure activates at Baltimore pier and harbour. As examples, he listed diving, sea angling and sailing. Sailing would appear to be particularly vibrant, not only with adults, but also with teenagers and younger children. Quoting Kieran in reference to his own family, “All our kids began sailing lessons when they were seven or eight years of age. They learned to sail, learned the Rules of the Road (international regulations for preventing collisions at sea) and became interested in the sea. At the age of sixteen or seventeen they completed the instructor’s course. Having worked for a time as assistant instructors, they later became fully fledged instructors. It’s great for kids.” He went on to say, “Since around the year 2000 an Easter time sailing programme, open to all interested 5th and 6th class national school pupils is on offer. Basically kids are invited to come along and partake in an introductory sailing course. Those who enjoy the experience have the option of returning in the summer to participate in a full sailing course. To the best of my knowledge 50 to 70 per cent of children in the local parish are currently learning to sail.”

So much for children and small boat sailing! When it comes to larger visiting yachts and motor cruisers, Kieran is of the opinion that facilities open to those vessels leaves much to be desired. While he didn’t spell out any particular area of improvement, I’m assuming that a breakwater and purpose built marina would be desirable.

A Step Up

What of the man himself? Is sailing expertise included in his seafaring repertoire? Not surprisingly, the answer is yes! His introduction came when as a student at Plymouth Nautical College he learned to sail a GP14. In more recent years he successfully completed the yacht masters' course at Poole, Somerset. Armed with an Offshore Certificate he is qualified to take a boat anywhere in the world up to 150 miles offshore. Not being too familiar with a yacht masters certificate, I asked if it were a prestigious qualification. Probably a stupid question to which Kieran answered, "Look, anyone that is into sailing or boating of any kind should go off and learn as much as possible about the sea" Right, I replied, and then asked what the course entailed. "It's made up of two parts, learning the Rules of the Road and a practical. During the practical you're observed by an examiner on your ability to 'work around a boat', followed by an examination on the Rules of the Road, e.g. familiarity with buoying system, tidal systems and secondary ports. A yacht master's certificate or equivalent qualification is a requirement for coxswains taking charge of RNLI lifeboats on passage, but not so to operate within a particular station range."

So does Kieran do leisure sailing? Again the answer is yes! He went on to say," I do a good bit sailing to places such as the Isles of Scilly and the French coast. In fact in a few days time, in the company of three others, I'm setting off from Cork on passage to La Rochelle on the west coast of France. I have also taken part in the Dun Laoghaire to Dingle race on a few occasions. My knowledge of navigation comes in very handy, especially on trips to the continent. It's something that I'm very interested in."

Thankfully there wasn't a lifeboat callouts during the several hours Kieran took from his busy schedule to converse with me. A most interesting and enjoyable evening at Baltimore!

P.S. More recently when I met Kieran we had two more recent developments to discuss, both pertaining to his lifeboat activities. Firstly, it was the rescue of sailors from a capsized yacht, and secondly the arrival at Baltimore Station of a brand new Tamar Class RNLI lifeboat.

The yacht incident involved the Baltimore RNLI lifeboat *Hilda Jarrett*, a boat privately owned and skippered by lifeboat deputy mechanic Jerry Smith, and the Irish Coast Guards. The rescue operation took place on August 15th 2011 off the West Cork coast when the 100ft yacht, *Rambler,* capsized during the Fastnet Race. Her crew members were in imminent danger of drowning. The high profile rescue of all received extensive media coverage when the Baltimore Lifeboat volunteer crew under Coxswain Kieran Cotter brought twenty of the rescued sailors safely ashore. Jerry Smith did likewise with four other crew members. A remaining crew member of the ill-fated yacht was airlifted to hospital by an Irish Coast Guard helicopter.

The RNLI Lifeboat *Alan Massey* – Photo credit RNLI.

The arrival of the new, the state-of-the-art Tamar Class, RNLI Lifeboat, *Alan Massey*, at Baltimore early in 2012, brought with it a great sense of satisfaction to the community as whole, but was obviously a bit special for Kieran. While the *Hilda Jarrett* served the Station well over many years, a modern replacement boat was probably overdue. The new 16.3 meters boat that has a speed potential of 25 knots, is Kieran says, "User-friendly, great to handle, but you need a lot of concentration at all times. Everything happens very fast, much faster than on the previous boat. It is her capability and speed to rescue that sets her apart. She definitely belongs to the modern age of lifeboats." Worthy of note is that between the new lifeboat and station improvements, the RNLI is committing between six and seven million euro to the Baltimore Station.

Good luck to the *Alan Massey* and all those brave volunteers who sail in her.

Dan Leonard

Dan Leonard at his Dunmore East home. Credit P. Nolan.

A 2010 July morning at Dunmore East! It's beautiful weather wise and the view out across the expanse of sea looking towards Hook Head is exquisite. As I stand at the Dock Road wall, I reflect on Dunmore East of the early 1950s when boats owned by my family were instrumental in pioneering the driftnet herring fishing of that era at the Co Waterford port. In the years that immediately followed, the influx of fishing boats, the unprecedented quantities of fish landed and the general upturn in hustle and bustle at the pier and beyond transformed Dunmore East from the quaint village I first came to know. Yet, that was merely the beginning, because the momentum gained in those early years increased to an unbelievable level throughout the 1960s and '70s.

On my current visit I arrived at a Dunmore East (Upper) that bore many of the characteristics observable in the early 1950s. While the village itself has expanded somewhat, the heart of it has not greatly changed. However, while the pier has taken on more expansive dimensions the level of activity there was minimal. Signs of the heady days remain in the form of fish auction halls and related buildings. Alas though, fish is no longer sold at what I believe was the main hall on the 'new pier'. Instead, the building which showed signs of dilapidation appeared to function in some capacity as an aqua adventure centre. A second auction hall with locked doors had just been deemed no longer fit for purpose. Nearby fish factories are closed down! While a cluster of half-deckers and other smaller vessels occupied one corner of the pier basin, only two substantial fishing vessels were otherwise on view. What a change from the days when boats crowded the port while other herring laden vessels queued outside waiting for a vacant space to land their catches. At what I refer to as 'the old pier' one had little difficulty in recalling nights of yesteryear. Nights when I stood looking down from the Dock Road on a hive of activity created by an assemblage of deck-lit luggers, each being loaded with barrelled herring for shipping to the continent! In order to facilitate, what were often chaotic landing situations during the day, lugger loading took place at night while the fishing fleet was at sea. Sadly, in the current state of inactivity, ghosts of the past stir up a palpable sense of 'what had been'. The wheel in many ways has turned full circle!

Leaving the nostalgia behind I decided to go and chat with some of the locals I have come to know one way and another. Among them are Dan Leonard and Sean O'Driscoll, both natives of the Island of Cape Clear but now long-time domicile and well settled at Dunmore East. Then there is Billy Power, a member of the widely know and highly respected Dunmore East business family that have supplied food and drink to the local population and fishermen from all quarters for almost as long as anyone can remember. The late Mrs Power, Billy's mother, affectionately known as, Katie, was an institution, and is fondly remembered by hundreds of fishermen who passed through for her generosity and maternal concerns. A man I spoke to on the street said, "Powers Bar has been there forever." I recall that when I first visited Dunmore East in the early 1950s, Powers combined the businesses of pub, grocery and butchery under the one roof. At least that's how I remember it! Somewhere along the way that scenario changed because today Power's Centra Convenience Store and the famous bar are now separate entities.

First I met up with Dan Leonard, a man I came to know when as the young boy he accompanied his father, Danny, on ferry and mail boat trips between Baltimore and Cape Clear. That was all of sixty plus years ago! In fairness I should add that Dan is somewhat my junior! While I was aware of him fishing on this boat and that, I must admit that it was many years later when I met up with his aunt, the late Sister Kieran, a Cross and Passion Order nun in Ballycastle, Co Antrim, that I learned of his highly successful fishing career. In more recent years I've renewed my acquaintance with him.

The *Caronia 11* leaving Baltimore following a refit. Credit Brendan Leonard

As we sat in his car on the pier at Dunmore East, Dan recalled his lifetime in fishing and lamented the fact that the industry is in decline. Now that he is retired from sea going his interest in commercial fishing hasn't diminished a single iota. Not only is he involved with the Irish South & East Fish Producers Organisation Ltd, but the Leonard family owned boat *Caronia 11*(W297) fishes out of Dunmore East. The elegant, 80ft, immaculately maintained, Danish built seiner, shore managed and maintained by Dan's son Brendan, makes four, five or six-day trips fishing off the south/south-west coast. Fish caught by the boat is landed at Dunmore East, the greater part of which is sold to Saltees Fish, Kilmore Quay, who in turn sell it on to Morgan's Fine Fish, Omeath, Co Louth, a company recognised as experts in quality seafood processing. The fish reaches the tables of diners in this country and possibly beyond through the retail and wholesale network built up over many years by the Morgan owned firm.

I steered Dan away from the present in order to concentrate a little on the past, and his rise to the outstanding and highly respected fisherman he became. When I asked about his early days in Cape Clear, without hesitation he answered, "Everyone belonging to me, on my mother's and father's side, going back generations were fishermen." He went on to say, "My first taste of fishing came while still of school going age when I worked ten lobster pots around the harbour in Cape during the summer months. Gradually I slipped into the traditional family way of life when as a teenager I began fishing on Joe Sheehan's *Ard Casta*. Later I fished on Johnny O'Driscoll's *Ros Maolan* before joining Donnchadh O'Driscoll on the *Radiance*. By then the time had come for me to acquire my own boat. I started off fishing lobster, crayfish and oysters with the 38ft *Puffin*, spending the early years working mainly up along the west coast. In 1967 I decided 'to go big' and bought the *Christine* (SO449) from Albert Swan, Killybegs, and renamed her *Golden Fort*. It was then that I joined forces with the late Tommy Power of Kilmore Quay who had a boat named *Alliance*. Thus a highly successful fishing partnership that was to last for years was born. The two boats did very well while herring pairing out of Dunmore, so much so, that it was a case of upwards and onwards. In 1971 I sold the *Golden Fort* to a Clogherhead man and purchased the Swedish built, 74ft, *Candy.* I renamed her *Brendette,* a combination derived from the names of Brendan and Deirdre, my son and daughter. At the same time Tommy Power had a new boat, the 75ft *Eilish Anne* (W27), built at Baltimore. Using the newly purchased boats Tommy and I successfully continued herring pairing until the compulsory closure of the Celtic Sea fishery. In 1983 I sold the *Brendette* to Michael Doran, Howth, and acquired my first seiner, the 75ft, Eyemouth built, *Dee Marie* (W448) (ex: *Burton Fleming*)."

With the *Dee Marie* Dan engaged in seining from the word go. That was all of twenty-eight years ago. He describes that period, "As the best days of my life." Of seining he says, "I should have been at it from the start. It's a great and gentle way of fishing, I loved seining. I made more money from whitefish while seining than I ever did from herring fishing; twice as much. You could walk on hake the first years we were out. At times we fished as far away as one hundred miles off the south-west coast. We were the only Irish boat fishing there then but we had foreigners for company. After three or four days out we would have around five hundred boxes aboard. We couldn't take anymore. We landed in Newlyn, Cornwall for nine years where market prices were far superior to those paid in Ireland. It used to take us twenty hours to steam home to Dunmore but it was worth it."

Dan had a special mention for the crews that accompanied him over the years at sea. I had he said, "Great men along with me. Behind every good skipper there has to be a good crew because the skipper is only as good as his crew. I was very fortunate to have such loyal, good, decent and able men. I would like to take this opportunity to thank all of those who worked with me down through the years. I'd a history of keeping crew for long periods, among them one man who spent twenty-eight-and-a-half years with me. Presently the *Caronia 11* has a full Irish crew. We have never had a problem with getting or keeping Irish crews."

In general conversation Dan expressed his immense disappointment at the way things have gone in the Irish fishing industry and particularity the decline of his home port. It's sad, he says, "To see the port here going. With the auction hall closed down and the harbour silting up, things are not looking good for the future. Because of the silting, boats can't get in and out at low water anymore. When I first came here in the 1960s there were up to two hundred people working on the pier. Jobs associated with the barrelling of herring and all that entailed were highly labour intensive. Then there were up to one hundred boats landing here, each with a crew of six men, that's six hundred in all. Add to that, agents, fish buyers, hauliers and various ancillary staff. In all there were up to one thousand individuals involved in the fishing industry at this port. There are very few now!"

Where did it all go wrong? What happened to an apparent developing industry that smacked of major national significance? Well, in a nutshell, Dan, in common with all fishermen I meet believes that the fault lies with a combination of ineptness, negativity, ignorance, hints of vindictiveness and a general disregard on the part of successive home governments. Couple that with a multitude of autocratic draconian directives handed down by E.U. Officials whose interest in furthering a fishing industry in this country is minimal. It's a virtually impossible task for fishermen to combat such odds.

Then I ask about fish stocks. The reply comes, "There is plenty of fish, and there is no scarcity here, definitely not! There was never as much herring as there is this year. We have a great fishery. If the market price for fish wasn't so poor and we could somehow work with the meagre quotas imposed. Bass are extremely plentiful off the south coast. In that case a strange anomaly exists; while we are allowed to catch them and have them on board, we're not allowed to land them! Meanwhile Belgium and the French trawlers are fishing the same species up to our limit and have no sales problem. Those people are laughing at us." Again in reflective mood, Dan says, "It's sad to see the way Dunmore has gone. Maybe someday it will make a comeback. The 1970s were very big here; fortunes were made."

Dan who retired from fishing some years ago says he would like to return to the job he so appreciated, "I love the sea, I love fishing", he says. While life has in many ways been very good to Dan, he has had the occasional setback, not least the untimely passing of his wife, Bernadette, some seventeen years ago. These days he obviously has a wonderful working relationship with his very businesslike son, Brendan. Great to see! A keen interest in forging links with descendants of people who left the south-east in the 1880s to take up fishing in Newfoundland has led Dan, in the company of sixty-three others, to visit the shores of the Canadian province. So well were they received that a visit by Newfoundlanders in the opposite direction was imminent at the time of my visit.

Dan is now a gentleman of leisure by any standards. His home overlooks the huge expanse of sea reaching to Hook Head and beyond. Before parting company we sat, drank a cup of tea, and chatted about this and that. So what does he do with his spare time now-a-days? Well apart from his interest in the comings and goings of the *Caronia 11*, he also, wait for it, is a keen ballroom dancer, a pastime that takes him to venues near and far. Then of course there is his pleasure cruiser based at Killaloe, Co Clare which he uses not only for visits to West Cork but also on occasional trips to the continent.

Just as I about to leave Dan's home on that July day, he spoke of how he believes the banning of salmon fishing around our coastline has led to fewer young men choosing fishing as a career. He feels that those few months spent on salmon boats during the summer led to many teenagers taking the next step that led to fulltime fishing; no such introduction to seagoing now exists!

Ciaran O'Regan

Ciaran O'Regan boarding *Grievous Angel* at Dingle Ferry Terminal. Cre P. Nolan.

On my way from Tralee to Dingle, Co Kerry, I took the very picturesque route via the Conor Pass – Ireland's highest mountain road. From the summit downwards, with the expanse of Dingle Bay in full view, a wide and sweeping road took me to the heart of the vibrant town that is apparently geared to cater for every whim of the thousands of tourists who visit throughout the summer months. A superb and extensive purpose built seafront area, that incorporates two vehicle parks, splendid piers, a marina centre, a boat charter terminal and a tourist office, is very impressive indeed. Sadly, I have to report that fishing boat activity at the pier was minimal. Several boats were tied up with little signs of regular sea going. Only one that was having gill nets hauled aboard showed signs of recent fishing. Truly, there was little to suggest that the vibrancy of the tourist industry was in any matched by local commercial fishing activity.

A peaceful scene at Dingle pier! The redundant weed covered slipway in the foreground is all that remains of the once vibrant boatyard. Credit P. Nolan.

At the ferry terminal I spotted Ciaran O'Regan, skipper of the *Grievous Angel,* a man whose father I knew many years ago. We chatted for awhile. Later, at his Ballydavid home, five miles west of Dingle, having been warmly welcomed by his wife Josephine, Ciaran began to tell me of his working lifetime experiences; mostly as a shipwright at the Dingle BIM Boatyard, but also an unforgettable period of his life when he played a major role in the building of *Jeanie Johnston*, a replica of the original 154ft (overall length) three-masted barque. His recall on the history of boat building at the Yard is noteworthy. The days when most of what went on in Dingle revolved around fishing and boat building are still deep-seated in his mind.

His boatyard recall goes back to the mid-1960s when his father, renowned boat builder John O'Regan was foreman at the Dingle BIM Boatyard – "I'd be hanging around the boatyard a lot at that time as a ten-year-old. The work force consisted of around fourteen men. They were mostly building 26ft clinker BIM boats. The boat names all began with the word *Cill,* e.g. *Cill Droma* and *Cill Moibhe.* Up to four of them were built simultaneously and stockpiled outside in the yard. I have a clear memory of six or seven boats undergoing trials in the Bay on the same day. There were also some 32ft boats and, I believe, two 30-footers built around that time. The 32-footers were known as *Beal* boats, again because of the naming format, all of which began with the word *Beal*, e.g. *Beal Tragha* and *Beal Atha.* The 30-footers, labelled *Islander Class* were carvel built 'double enders'. The building of those three different types of boat accounted for the work that went on in the boatyard between 1964 and '69."

Ciaran is aware that between 1954 and '64 the Dingle BIM Boatyard built 50-footers only. During that period there were eighteen of the extremely popular vessels built, beginning with the Paddy & Tommy Devane owned, *Ros Glas* (D432), and ending with Sonny Brosnan's *Ros Beithe* (D44). Building of 50-footers recommenced in 1969! By the end of 1970 three boats were completed, *St Peter* (D508), *St Anne* (T9) and *St Colette* (T49), with the final boat going to the O'Connell brothers at Cahirciveen.

In October 1970 at the age of fifteen Ciaran joined the boatyard as an apprentice shipwright. Building of 52ft fishing boats, one was in fact 53ft, with cruiser sterns and soft-nosed stems (Tyrrell type) had just begun. In the years that immediately followed five or six were completed. In the July 1971, the 53ft boat *Midnight Star* was issued to the Moore family, Killybegs. She was rigged for seining and was basically the same as the 52-footers with an extra frame. The 52-footers built were the *Foyle Fisher* (May 1970) for the McClenaghan family at Greencastle, the *Artic Swan* (October 1970) for a Skerries owner, and the *Silver Fern* (March 1971) for George Corr, Loughshinney. Ciaran is of the opinion that while those boats were a few feet longer and a 'bit beamier', they had much the same draft as the 50-footers, and were really not any great improvement on them.

He recalls going on a maiden voyage up the east coast on the *Silver Fern* when on her way to participate in the *World Fishing Exhibition* held at Dublin in 1971. Funny he says what sticks in your mind, "Newly built boats from other yards were also on show at Dun Laoghaire, which is where the fishing boats were exhibited. I remember that we tied up beside George Rogan's Killybegs built, 58ft *Golden Sunset* (D535) and thinking what a monster of a boat she seemed compared to the *Silver Fern.* Of course she wasn't but at the time to me she was. Then along came Tommy Power's (Kilmore Quay) 75ft *Eilish Anne* (W27), a boat just completed at the Baltimore BIM Yard. She really dwarfed our little 52-footer."

As the 1970s progressed a number of boats ranging in length from 54ft upwards were built at the Dingle Boatyard. The first 58-footer, *Sean Og* (D551), issued in March 1972 went to Kirwans at Clogherhead. Two further 58-footers, the *Miraculous* (D603) (December 1972), and the *Sharon Rose* (December 1973) were built for Skerries owners. Another 58-footer, the *Bountiful* (August 1972) was issued to Brendan Gill, Greencastle. Other boats issued around that time were the 54ft *Assumpta* (May 1973) and the 56ft *Favourite* (December 1971) respectively to Patsy Griffin, Dingle and James Gallagher, Burtonport. Recalling names and details of boats built all those years ago had Ciaran's mind working overtime. Nevertheless, he soldiered on and remembered that in 1974 the first 65ft boat was built at the Yard. She was he said, "The *Darnette* (SO503) for Michael Gallagher, Burtonport. The same man, I believe, previously had the 50-footer *Rath Osan* (D208) and the aforementioned *Favourite* built at Dingle." At the time of writing the *Rath Osan*, owned by Sean Kelly is still fishing out of Helvick while the *Favourite* owned by J&S Moore Fishing Ltd., Killybegs had just been decommissioned. Ciaran went on to say, "We built four 65-footers, three of which went to Burtonport owners - *Autumn Glory* (SO520) (September 1974), the *Onedin* (April 1975), and the *Saint Oliver* (SO601) (December 1975). The fourth boat, *Roving Swan,* went to local man Patrick Sheehy. Issued respectively in September 1976 and April 1977, were the 70ft *Silver Spruce* (W125) to Niko Murphy, Dunmore East, and the 60ft *Sea Eagle* (SO637) to a Killybegs owner."

In November 1978 the first transom stern 65ft boat, *Aelindrew* (SO687) built at the Yard, was issued to the Fallon family of Achill Island. In Mach 1979, John Corrigan also of Achill Island took delivery of the *Specked Fort*, the second and only other transom stern boat to be built at Dingle during BIM's tenure. Ciaran explained, "Naval architect Maurice Napier (of Mc Caig and Napier, Glasgow), designed those 65ft boats; they were heavy and very deep for their size. They had 12ft draft. Later we did build two boats in excess of 70ft, one of 72.5ft and another of 75ft. Really our maximum building capability at the Dingle Yard was 70ft. Of the three BIM Boatyards ours was the smallest."

As the 1980s closed in, 'times they were a changing' in the fishing industry, and with that change came more powerful engines and stronger built boats. The mid-water boats were towing bigger nets and consequently greater engine power was required. Gone for the most part were the days of the 152hp Gardner!

Ciaran, now thinking aloud when recalling those distant days, said, "When we were building 70-footers, the other BIM Yards at Killybegs and Baltimore were building 80 and 86-footers. They were massive timber boats, too big in my opinion. I believe that timber boat size should not have exceeded 70ft. Over that length, lack in rigidly became a problem and as a result they became prone to leaking – the overall weight of the boat became too much. The fact is that hulls of lengthy timber boats, especially those with transom sterns, are straight sided for the most part. This has a weakening effect on planking when compared to shorter curvier hulls of boats such as the 50 or 56-footers; basically curved timber planking is more rigid."

"Worthy of note is that by the late 1970s steel had crept in as a component part of 'timber boats'. Actually, it began in the late 1960s with steel engine beds, and then moved on to steel bulkheads in the early 1970s. By the mid to late 1970s steel deck beams were being fitted. As a result I believe that boats were greatly improved in terms of strength – gone were the leaks around decks that were common in lengthy boats with timber beams. Steel deck structures were also to manifest themselves in the form of whalebacks, shelter decks and wheelhouses. Slowly but surely 'timber fishing boats' became vessels of steel in all but the actual hull. An indication of the advent of the all- steel boat came, when in the late 1970s and early '80s shipwrights were sent on welding courses, and a requirement for all apprentices from the late 1970s onwards was to have welding as part of their training."

Many years ago I remember my father-in-law using the expression, 'the writing's on the wall,' to describe an evitable situation – like for example that I was planning to marry his daughter. I'm not sure how happy he was about that particular inevitability; I think it got his blessing, but that's another story. In the case of large timber built fishing boats, as Ciaran has so eloquently outlined, 'the writing was definitely on the wall' as the early 1980s approached. They were fast becoming a thing of the past! As a result BIM interest in the Dingle Boatyard ceased. However, that was not the end of boat building at the Yard! Ciaran explained ,"Joe Boyle, the incumbent manager, formed his own company and with a reduced workforce we began building transom stern boats ranging in length from 56ft to 60ft – dependent on the number of frames. We built four of those boats in all. The first, a 56-footer, *Marber Therese* (T61), was built for Mickey Devane, Portmagee. He wanted a multi-purpose boat, one suitable for trawling, mid-watering and importantly for potting. Incidentally, he later told me that he regretted not getting a much bigger boat at the time as he greatly enjoyed mid-watering, and in any case potting with larger boats was beginning to die out. The second of those boats, *Paul Stephen* (SO746*),* was built for Gerard Gill, Greencastle, another one went to a Killybegs owner, while the fourth, *Atlantic Fisher,* found a first home at Dingle under the ownership of Tom Kennedy. While the latter is still Dingle based, she is not to be confused with a boat of the same name, also owned by Tom Kennedy, but is a 72ft Scotch built gill netter, registration number T116, and currently the largest timber built boat fishing out of Dingle."

Ciaran continued with his recall, "The late 1980s saw a further reduction in the workforce at the boatyard; I believe that latterly we were down to two shipwrights and a welder. As if to defy logic we undertook to build what I believe was one of the largest boats built at the yard in any era - a massive undertaking! She was the 73ft *Silver Harvester* (B713) built for James McClements, Portavogie. At the time she was one of only two boats in this country fitted with mackerel carrying tanks. Sadly, she was the last boat to be built at Dingle Boatyard; orders simply dried up. Steel built boats were becoming the order of the day, and anyway with timber getting scarce the cost of building boats became prohibitive. It's true that we had lasted longer than most yards. While we continued for a time to do some repair work, it was limited because our facilities were primarily geared for building."

By then the building of steel boats was well established at Tyrrells of Arklow, the New Ross Boatyard and Killybegs Boatyard (then run by Tyrrells). Ciaran has specific memories of ongoing work at Killybegs. He recalled that, "Three or four steel boats of around 50ft were built there. Those were followed by two beautiful and well constructed 90ft boats, creations of well known designer Hugo van der Zwan. I worked with him at Dingle when he designed steel wheelhouses for boats we built there. The first such wheelhouse was built for the previously mentioned John Corrigan's *Speckled Fort*. Because it was all new to us at the time he supervised the building of it. In addition to designing many Arklow built boats, he also designed at least one tank boat destined for Killybegs in fairly recent years."

Today, the only sign that a boat building yard existed at Dingle is the sight of a weed covered, derelict slipway that looks completely out of place in the modern complex.

So the Dingle Boatyard closed down and for all intent and purposes Ciaran was out of a job. While he did dabble in repair work, there wasn't enough of it. He was then around forty years of age. So what was he to do? Commercial fishing at Dingle was in a state of flux. He remembered when growing up in the 1960s that in addition to the 50-footers and other boats there were seven, eight, or maybe nine 56-footers fishing out of Dingle. The buzz around the pier and town, he said, "Was unbelievable." Yes indeed, "Boats were landing up to 100 boxes fish per day." That situation had largely died out! Nevertheless, he decided to give fishing a go. He tried his hand at the salmon, did a bit of trawling and mid-watering, but he said, "I made no money." Importantly though, he enjoyed it! I was he said, "Too old by then, you'd want to own your own boat at that stage. I did enjoy myself and found fishing very interesting. As a shipwright I had spent years telling fishermen where they should put this and that in their boats, but had not actually seen my suggestions followed through in a working environment. Now I had the opportunity! However long-term fishing as an occupation was not for me."

Sails at the ready as the *Jeanie Johnston* leaves port.

Coincidentally, following the closure of the Dingle Boatyard a syndicate based at Tralee, Co Kerry were hatching plans to have a replica of the 19th century three masted barque *Jeanie Johnston* built. The original ship was completed in Quebec, Canada in 1847 by the Scottish born shipbuilder John Munn. Purchased at Liverpool by Tralee based merchants John Donovan & Sons she successfully traded between Ireland and North America for a number of years, engaged mainly in transporting emigrants from

Ireland and returning with cargos of timber. It was at a time when the effects of the great famine were devastating the population of Ireland.

Of significance to the current building project was that the replica should be built at Blennerville, Tralee, Co Kerry because it was from there that the original *Jeanie Johnston* made her maiden voyage in 1848. The man appointed to manage the actual building of the ship was Michael O'Boyle, a retired foreman of Killybegs BIM Boatyard. The job criteria of overseeing the building of one of the most ambitious maritime heritage projects ever undertaken in Ireland included the assembly of an experienced workforce and the sourcing of necessary materials. While talking to Michael about project a few years back, he told me that once appointed his main priority was to get knowledgeable and experienced personnel to work along with him. The men he said, "That immediately came to mind were the O'Regan brothers, Ciaran and Peter. From the days I spent at Dingle Boatyard I knew them to be men of outstanding commitment, with superb shipyard qualities and an all round acumen that is rarely found. To persuade them to come onboard was my only problem! I contacted them and even though neither had applied for any job to do with the project, to my enormous relief I met with success. I knew immediately that between us we had the capability of seeing the project through; once I had them along with me I knew I would be alright. Their input was to prove invaluable."

On my meeting with Ciaran he recalled the circumstances of his initial involvement with the *Jeanie Johnston* project as outlined by Michael. That it was a massive undertaking was clear to all of us, but as Michael pointed out, it was a chance of a lifetime, adding, "Sure we can only do our best." The ship was to be built at Blennerville on what was at the outset a green-field site. When Ciaran arrived on the scene a workshop had been built but there were no doors or windows in it, and power was provided by generators. However in time the workshop was completed, and with *mains power* installed, they started cutting frames for the ship. Ciaran recalled, "A similar project was ongoing at New Ross Drydock where a replica of another three masted barque, the *Dunbrody* (originally built at Quebec in 1845), was being built. She was framed and maybe half planked when we started cutting frames for the *Jeanie Johnston*. The timbers in both vessels were comparable. While the *Dunbrody* was a slightly fuller and beamier boat, and designed by different men, basically the work in building was the same."

To cut the frames, the '*Jeanie Johnston* company' purchased a flat belt driven band saw that had been idle at Tyrrells of Arklow for years. Apparently it was the saw used to cut the frames for the *Asgard*. Peter O'Regan, who Michael O'Boyle described as 'brilliant' when it came to mechanical work of any kind converted the band saw to V-belt driven. He also credited Peter with having a great talent for breathing new life into old and very sick pieces of machinery. The V-belt conversion made an enormous difference to the cutting power of the saw. Ciaran went on to say, "We spent a couple of months cutting the frames, starting off purposely with the most difficult, that is, the one with the greatest bevel. We reckoned that if we could do that the others should not present any big problem." As an afterthought he recalled, "One day a retired Tyrrell Boatyard man who visited us at Blennerville had a tear in his eye as he watched the band saw in action; he couldn't believe that the saw he had worked with for years was now capable of cutting timber of such dimensions. He approached Ciaran, introduced himself and said, "Jack Tyrrell used to have me standing on top of the jockey pulley in order to increase tension on the belt when we were cutting frames. There you are now cutting much heavier frames with little or no fuss." Additionally, a smaller band saw that originated from a Blennerville workshop and found its way to the Dingle boatyard, returned to Blennerville to help out with the current project. It had a tilting head and was used for cutting lighter timber.

Ciaran continued to explain progress as follows, "With the frames ready we started off with the deadwood and keel (all Irish oak). Next we positioned the frames. The designer had drawn the lines, and with good lofting and band sawing, when stood upright it appeared as if the frames had been chipped and scudded – they all lined up perfectly. That particular work was done out in the open! It was only when the framing was completed that a shed was built around the ship. We had spent a very cold winter working outside! Now inside the new shed we began planking – larch on oak. However, work soon more or less came to a halt. A problem arose because of difficulty in bending the larch used. Due to the scarcity of Irish larch we had sourced some overseas. Unfortunately it proved to be unsuitable!

During the layoff Michael O' Boyle was left with no alternative but to travel to Austria in search of suitable timber. Somewhere in the Alpine slopes on sight he identified the exact trees required for the job. It turned out to be beautiful timber, perfect larch to work with. Planking then went ahead quickly with very little breakage. The first plank to go on was the aft starboard garboard. Over the space of a couple frames the *after end* changed from vertical to around 15 degrees off the horizontal, yet I couldn't believe how easy we got the plank in." An idea of what was involved can be gleaned from the following – the approximate plank dimensions were 40ft X 28/30in X 5in. It was in the steam pot for about seven hours. Normally planks were steamed on the basis of an hour per inch of thickness plus one additional hour. In this case a further extra hour was given. With steaming completed it required about twenty men to remove the plank from the pot and transfer it to the ship as quickly as possible. The whole operation had previously been well rehearsed –each man had a specific job to do. Ciaran recalls, "When the time came, 4.45pm to be specific, excitement ran high amongst all present as the plank was removed from the steam pot and taken to the vessel. We were so engulfed in steam that sweat poured off us. It was a 'big moment', the first plank was about to go on! By 5pm it was a case of mission accomplished – the plank was cramped in perfectly, absolutely perfectly. The whole operation was completed in fifteen minutes. One of the shipwrights suggested that we start nailing; no I said it's perfect now, we'll do that in the morning. So carried away was he by our success that he turned to me and said, you know what Ciaran this is better than sex, it was just amazing."

Elated by our achievement, there was only one way to unwind. I said to the men, "Come on we'll all go for a few pints. Around thirty of us headed off to the local pub. I ordered a pint for all present. Four rounds later I was still ordering. At that point I said to the lads we'll have to start paying for our own from now on. The barman enquired as to who was paying for the 120 or so pints he had served. I told him to make out a bill to the '*Jeanie Johnston* company'. We finished up the night good and merry. Nothing like a celebration! All was fine until about two months later when I was called to a meeting by the company and asked to explain what this pub bill was about. In response, I enquired, "Have you paid it?" The reply was, no, but we will! However we want to know what authority you had to run up this bill. I told them I decided to do it myself in way of celebrating the first plank being successfully fitted to the ship without a hitch of any kind. I went on to say that if we had broken the plank it would have cost them ten times the amount of the bill. What's more the men appreciated the gesture! It proved to be a marvellous bonding exercise, the value of which was evident in the spirit with which they carried out their jobs in subsequent months. A measure of the enthusiasm can be judged from the fact that six or seven additional planks were fitted to the vessel. I added that we would be having a repeat celebration when the last plank – *the whiskey plank* - went on. In fairness all was accepted by 'the powers that be' without a problem of any kind.

From there on, under the watchful eyes of Michael O'Boyle and Ciaran, bit by bit, the great ship *Jeanie Johnston* slowly but surely took shape. Ciaran said, "We built the ship the way we were taught to build a boat. The job brought with it immense personal satisfaction. At times we were under pressure to go about the job in different ways but we never veered from our own way. The hull was designed but when it came to building and fitting her out she tended to be designed as we went along – there was a bit of chopping and changing. As mentioned already it was a massive undertaking and indeed there were occasional problems. In fairness to our employers, we were provided with great facilities in the way of workshops, proper lifting gear and so on."

The *Jeanie Johnston*, whose dimensions and other details read as follows, extreme length 45m (148ft); overall length 37.5m (123ft); bean 8m (26ft); draft 4.2m (14ft); displacement 510 tonnes; 3-masted barque was launched via pontoon barge at Blennerville in 2002. A year or so later the ship was completely fitted out and the dream hatched by the syndicate years previously came to fruition when she sailed from Fenit, Co Kerry across the Atlantic to the USA and Canada. She returned to Ireland having stopped off at over twenty ports. One other detail is that nationals of eleven different countries were employed in the Yard workforce during the project.

When the '*Jeanie project*' came to an end Ciaran returned to carrying out small boat repairs for awhile. By then fishing at Dingle had further declined, but lo and behold the tourist industry was very much on the way up. With the upturn came employment opportunities! The offshore islands and the adjacent sea area were becoming popular eco-tourist attractions so Ciaran decided to have a go at the passenger ferry business. Suffice to say he is still ploughing the waters off the west Kerry coast while eager tourists experience the splendours of the Blasket Islands and Dingle Bay surroundings.

We chatted long into the evening at the O'Regan family home at Ballydavid. The day which began dull and murky had brightened up considerably; so much so that one could not fail to notice the outstanding seaward view out to the west. When I remarked as much, Ciaran said, "You need to see it as the sun slowly drops in the sky on an evening in high summer. The sun seems to get stronger as it makes its way downwards before disappearing in the deep blue yonder. We often sit at the front door until ten o'clock at night just taking in the magnificent vista that lay before us." Looking at it on that not so perfect evening I imagined the scene he described – a wonderful location!

On arrival at the O'Regan home earlier in the afternoon I noticed a very smart Beneteau motor cruiser, INIS, on a trailer in the yard. I was later to learn that she is owned by Ciaran's sons Paul and Michael. Paul, who was present, is obviously very proud of the immaculately maintained boat, and why not, she's a beauty. On a trip around to Baltimore she had performed splendidly. No doubt there will be many more enjoyable trips!

My visit to Ballydavid, as with visits to many men of the sea, went on longer than anticipated – so much to talk about! In Ciaran's case, with both parents hailing originally from Baltimore direction, my own place of birth, we had even more than is usual in common to talk about. His mother, who is a sister of the esteemed Leonard boat building family of yesteryear, Peter (late of Dingle) and Tim (Malahide), hailed from Reengaroga (just across the harbour from Baltimore), still lives in Dingle, and in spite of her advanced years walks off down the street to do her daily shopping.

The time had come to call it a day. Visiting Ciaran and his family had indeed been a great pleasure.

John Norris

John Norris at his home in Schull – 2011. Credit P. Nolan

I've been on boats since I could walk – the words of John Norris, now a retired skipper and ex-boat owner who lives at Schull, Co Cork. Born on Sherkin Island, John spent his national school holidays lobster fishing around the Island and Baltimore Harbour with his father, George, on the 20 ft boat *Parnell.* With school days behind him and shortly after his fourteenth birthday, John joined the crew of the *Marie*, a 32ft half-decker owned by fellow islander, John Beamish. The spring mackerel fishing season was about to begin. That he says, "Was my first venture at *deep sea* fishing, and what a tough old job mackerel fishing on a boat of that size was." As the youngest crew member it was John's tedious and miserable job during net hauling to coil the springback. The springback was a heavy and often tarred rope that stretched the full length of the nets, maybe up to a mile, depending on the number of nets used. The coiling was carried out in a semi-dark confined space and required to be ever so neatly done. It was every young man's nightmare, especially those who were subject to seasickness. John has vivid memories of that particular experience. Nevertheless he persevered!

As the years moved on John needed a job during the winter months when there was little or no fishing ongoing. A grant aided agricultural scheme came to the rescue. The scheme was a government initiative put in place to encourage the spreading of sea sand on farmland. Beaches on the west side of Sherkin Island became an important source of the soil nutrient for the local area. However, it had to be manually shovelled onto a horse cart at a strand and then transported 2km or so to a pier on the east side of the island. There it was tipped out before being manually shovelled into a sand boat - an open beamy vessel of comparatively low draft and fitted with an inboard engine. The vessel was capable of transporting loads of ten to twelve tons. With the load onboard and the tides suitable the boat set off to a destination, frequently eight miles up the Ilen River to Skibbereen. There, the sand to be later collected by farmers was manually shovelled on to a quay. The entire operation as outlined above was carried out by two men – John and the boat owner, Sean Connolly. It was extremely laborious work! When I remarked as much, John replied, "We didn't take any notice of it, but you wouldn't find many in their mid-teens to do it nowadays. I worked on the sand boat for three winters."

The first opportunity to venture into what John described as 'big-time fishing' came his way in June 1956 when the late Peter Downey, skipper and owner of the Baltimore based *Ros Droichead,* asked if I were interested in becoming a crew member. Acceptance meant that over the following three or so years he experienced fishing practices that 50ft boats of that era partook in; with occasional minor deviations it was whitefish seining from springtime through to late autumn, the remainder of the year was spent herring fishing. A typical seine-fishing-week, involved setting out from Baltimore at around 6am on Monday, landing in Castletownbere or Schull each evening during the week and returning to Baltimore late on Friday night. While Saturday might be spent checking out gear or carrying out jobs relating to the boat, Sunday was for the most part sacrosanct – a day off! When the time came to go in search of herring the routine changed greatly; no longer as case of regular daytime fishing. With Dunmore East established as the herring centre on the Irish coast and beyond, that was the place to go. It meant spending several weeks or even months away from the home base. John's introduction to herring fishing involved the 'coil-a-side' technique. He recalls that they first went to Dunmore East, to go seining off 'The Ship' (Coningingbeg Lightship), where plaice and other flatfish were plentiful. However, it soon became apparent that most boats were engaged in 'coil-a-side' herring fishing, so we decided to have a go at that. Soon that rather unorthodox technique was replaced by 'ringing'."

A Step Up

Following the years spent on the *Ros Droichead*, John, then around 21 years of age, in partnership with the late Danny O'Regan, Schull, a man he describes as, "A great friend", purchased the 50ft mfv *Marie de Montfort*, a boat fitted out for herring ringing. The *Marie de Montfort*, under John's guiding hand, pair- fished during the winter, trawled in the spring, and engaged in lobster fishing during the summer months. He recalls, "Trawling for herring at Dunmore East and later getting boat loads of whiting off Helvick." The lobster fishing mainly came about through links with Sherkin Island man Willie McCarthy, owner and skipper of the BIM 50-footer *Inis Arcain*. John recalls that, "Willie used to fish around the north Kerry coast and that encouraged me to go and give it a try." He went on to remark, "What crayfish and lobsters were there then! We were fishing 120 barrel pots, split into four strings and on a fine week we could land up to 100 dozen fish. When fishing anywhere around Tralee Bay, all 120 pots had to be taken aboard each night because of the presence of deadly nocturnal fish eating insects in the water. Once darkness fell they stripped the bait from the pots in a matter of minutes. That problem did not arise when fishing around Kerry Head or Loop Head. Barrel pots used at the time were very effective in catching big crayfish; some of those crayfish were huge, especially ones caught at the north side of Loop Head, along the coast to Kilkee, and around Rossbeigh. We regularly landed fish at The Maharees (Co Kerry) where we frequently anchored at night and also moored our storage tanks. It was there too that Dingle man Sonny Long bought and collected the fish for export. Those were the days! Among other factors, the use of gill and tangle nets contributed greatly to the demise of crayfish, and lobsters to a lesser extent."

Around the mid-1960s a decision was taken to trade in, as it were, the *Marie de Montfort* and the *Brightmoney* (another 50/51ft boat in which Danny O'Regan had an interest) for the Forbes of Sandhaven built, traditional 70ft Scotch mfv *Fairweather*. Southern Marine Ltd, Malahide, facilitated the deal. John fished on the *Fairweather* for three years. Then at the age of twenty-eight he decided to go it alone and get his own boat. He went back to Southern Marine and purchased a standard British Admiralty 65ft motor fishing vessel which he named *Water Lily*, after a boat owned by his grandfather on Sherkin Island in the distant past. She was powered by a 152hp Gardner engine, and was fitted out for trawling. By that time herring ringing was a thing of the past and had been replaced by mid-watering. John said, "My first mid-watering experience was pairing with the *Fairweather*, skippered by fellow Sherkin Island native, Jim O'Driscoll (Baxie). We spent a couple of winters successfully herring fishing around the south-east coast, landing at Dunmore East and Cobh. When that pairing partnership ended, I joined forces with the Tommy McGrath owned Dunmore East boat *Accord* – a boat similar to the *Fairweather*. We worked together for a winter or two herring fishing out of Dunmore East."

The decommissioned *Breda Helen* leaving Schull for scrapping at Ghent. Credit J. Norris.

Obviously things had gone well over the years for John because in 1972 he decided to go really big and he took delivery of the brand new Baltimore built 70ft *Breda Helen.* With a broad smile on his face, John says, "I suppose it was mad at the time, it was a big undertaking. The boat cost £1000 per foot. The actual overall cost was £70,240. He went on to say, "We started off trawling with the *Breda Helen.* Then during that first year we teamed up with the *Green Eagle*, a 75ft Norwegian built boat, owned and skippered by Pat O'Driscoll, Cape Clear. In the years that immediately followed we paired for herring at various locations, including the Irish Sea and Isle of Man in August/September, before heading back to Dunmore East for the start of the winter season there. We also fished locally around the Stags. It was when Pat got an even bigger boat that incompatibility of vessel sizes forced our partnership to end."

Life had to go on, and with pairing really being the main show in town, it was a case of finding another boat to work with. It came in the form of the *Una Alan,* a new 70ft boat built at the Baltimore BIM Yard for Castletownbere man Peter Carlton. During the period of that partnership the boats fished the south and west coasts. John recalls that during the couple of winters spent together they worked, "Up the west coast as far as Galway, here and there locally and also out of Dunmore East until the fishery was closed down." He went on to say that, "We got a lot of herring around the Blasket Islands and off Kerry Head. Lots of fish were landed in Fenit."

A Step Up

There was obviously a great deal of fluidity were fishing partnerships were concerned. The frequency of changes suggests as much. The *Breda Helen/Una Alan* venture lasted a few seasons, to be replaced by similar arrangements with first, the Castletownbere boat *Breda Annette* owned and skippered by Billy O'Driscoll, and later with Schull boat *Ocean Breeze* owned and skippered by Michael O'Driscoll. Sandwiched between two spells with the *Ocean Breeze* were three seasons with the Minihane owned, *Girl Geraldine*. Of pairing with the *Ocean Breeze,* John had this to say, "I spent a good many years working with the Michael O'Driscoll's *Ocean Breeze*. We fished very well together; we did very well indeed and were often the first boats in Dunmore with our quota."

However, as the saying goes, 'time and tide wait for no man'. John was no exception, and as he put it, "All of a sudden the years were beginning to run out on me." Fishing was becoming very much a young man's job and as such I was pleased that my son George joined the crew after doing his Leaving Certificate Examination. In time he took charge of the boat and fished her for ten or twelve years. For awhile I fished on her during the herring fishing seasons but eventually gave up completely. George continued trawling for a few years. But the world of fishing was rapidly changing in so many ways! The *Breda Helen*, while in great order, was no longer a young boat and was quickly becoming obsolete! Then a scrapping grant came on line; it was to be a one off! George decided to go for it with a view to maybe getting a newer boat at a later date. As things worked out the latter did not materialise."

On an autumn day in 2008 John along with his sons George and Sean set out from Schull for the last time on the *Breda Helen*. For company they had John O'Regan's *Carrigeen Bay*. Later they met up with a Galway boat off the Smalls. All three vessels were on their way to be scrapped in Belgium. An item on an internet website under the heading, *Breda Helen – Irish twin rigger scrapped at Van Heyghen, Recycling, Ghent*, gives the following interesting piece of information *–Breda Helen (S144) was scrapped in Ghent last October, but her bridge was saved from the breakers beasty machine. Now the bridge is placed on board the Venus (Z568) for her second life.*

So what does a fit and healthy John do with himself nowadays? Well he has an 18ft sailing boat without which he says, "I would be lost. I potter around in and out of Cape Clear and so on." He also has a wider interest in sailing and as a member of Schull Harbour Sailing Club participates in cruiser racing most Saturdays from May to September. As an afterthought he added, "I also sailed whenever possible during my fishing days and have owned my own sailing boat for about twenty-five years."

When I asked John if he had any memorable moments from his fishing days, he thought about it a little before recalling an incident that took place in the Dursey Sound. I'm sure that most people reading this column will be familiar with that particular oft-times nasty, south-west coast passage, but just in case, let me say that it is a narrow stretch of water which separates Dursey Island from the mainland. It is well known to seafarers as having a very strong tidal race and lying off centre on the mainland side is a reef of rocks which is submerged at high water – not the kind of place to be taken lightly in poor weather conditions. Well, on one particular night when John was mid-watering with a partner, herring markings appeared right in the middle of the sound (below the cable car that links the mainland to the island). It was John says, "A bad enough old night and somewhat reluctantly I went along with the decision to shoot the net." The boats were to tow north through the sound and then tow back in the opposite direction. On the north to south tow John's boat was on the island side, very close to shore, with the other boat on the mainland side. Here's how John recalls the subsequent happenings, "We were towing away when suddenly the other boat landed on a rock or rocks. As the swell went and came she rolled two or three times as if pivoted. I had no option but to keep going on because if I stopped my boat's starboard towing wires would have swung her bow around and being so close to the rock face a collision would have been inevitable. Meanwhile, a bigger than normal swell came in and to our enormous relief lifted the other boat off the rocks. Away we went south without the net getting caught. With the gear hauled we headed for Castletownbere where our partner's boat filled with water. She was later to undergo substantial repairs. That night I experienced the biggest fright of my entire fishing career." He went on to add that boats used to tow through the sound but in his opinion it was not an advisable thing to do; a bit dodgy!

Another mishap he recalled was falling overboard while seining west of Mizen Head on the *Ros Droichead*, "Fortunately it was a fine day with a virtually flat calm sea. I was picking up fish from the deck and slipped. Out I went over the rail and landed on the flat of my back in the water. One of the crew observed what had happened. The skipper immediately took the engine out of gear and allowed the boat to drop back to where I was. Quickly I was got hold of and unceremoniously hauled back in over the rail. While I suppose it could have been serious enough, it still didn't register on the same scale as the later Dursey Sound incident."

Meeting up with John and Ursula, both of whom I knew many moons ago when I lived in Baltimore, was a delight. As I left the house we stood for some time looking seawards and discussed the splendid panoramic view and allure of the various off shore islands. Then it was time for me to head off for Union Hall where I was staying over the weekend. My chat with the very amiable John brought back many memories and enlightened me as to what he had got up to over the years in the world of fishing.

Dick Power

Dick Power at his Dunmore East home – 2012. Credit P.Nolan

It was a fine summer's morning at Dunmore East. I had arranged to meet Dick on his return from an early morning mackerel fishing trip. As he has done since 2005, he occupies himself by fishing the *Dove*, a fibreglass boat of 6.87m length. While I waited on the pier a number of other small boats landed modest catches. An hour or later, comfortably seated at Dick's home on the outskirts of the village he was happy to recall his extensive fishing experiences. Experiences that spanned back all the way to early teenage years.

Dick is a native of Tramore Co Waterford. In 1943 he was born into a family long associated with commercial fishing. While his father spent some years in the Merchant Navy, for the most part he fished half-deckers out of Tramore. Later he spent time on boats owned by John Roche, Dunmore East. In the first instance he fished on the 38ft *St Joseph* before taking charge of the *Dun Beg*, a boat newly built at Skinner's Yard, Baltimore. It was during that period Dick came to live at Dunmore East.

A significant milestone was reached in Dick's early life when circa 1955 his father, widely known as William Butler Power, moved on from the *Dun Beg* and purchased the Portavogie built, 50ft seiner, *Golden Quest,* from a Kilkeel owner. This is how Dick remembers the sequence of events that followed, "My father started off lobster fishing with the *Golden Quest* in the summer of 1955 and later that year turned to seine netting, mostly for whiting, out of Helvick. I joined the crew a year later during the winter of 1956/'57." Around that time the Dunmore East herring bonanza was in its infancy and Helvick was also beginning to grow in stature as a seining port. Many boats working out of Dunmore engaged in the well-known 'coil-a-side' practice. However, the *Golden Quest*, which did not have an echo sounder fitted, remained based at Helvick. Without a sounder there was no point in trying to fish for herring. William and his crew continued seine netting with poor enough returns.

At the end of a prolonged lean period, mainly due to bad weather, with William wondering what to do next, a stroke of good luck came his way. It was triggered by the arrival of the boats, *Green Pastures* and *Green Hill*, (respectively owned and skippered by the Annalong brothers, Victor and Jack Chambers), to fish out of Helvick. During a boat to boat conversation William expressed his concerns to Jack, who advised him to stay put, saying, "There are loads of fish here off the bottom and they will be caught when the weather settles." That," Dick said, "is how it worked out. When the weather did settle, there was loads of fish there. From my memory, the fishing started about March and went on for about a month or so. We caught cod, plaice and whiting in quantities greater than we could handle. Indeed we did better than the boats that went to Dunmore herring fishing. "

The *Arctic Moon* and *Elizmor* at Dungarvan Quay – 1950s. Image Courtesy of Waterford County Museum.

In the years that immediately followed, herring ringing became prominent. Classy Scotch built ringers such as the *Arctic Moon* and *Elizmor,* owned and skippered respectively by the Matt Sloan and Eddie McEwen of Girvan, showed the way. Local owned boats that Dick remembered being involved at an early stage were the *Kittiwake* owned by Jack McGrath, Dunmore East and the *Kestrel* owned by John Hearne, Fethard-on-Sea, Co Wexford. While still a crew member on the *Golden Quest* he also remembers that they joined forces herring fishing with two other boats, the *Virginia* and the *Kittiwake* owned either then or later by Tommy McGrath, Dunmore East. The amount of herring there he said, "Was incredible, more ring nets than enough burst with the sheer weight of fish."

Circa 1959 the Power family acquire a second boat; the Herd & McKenzie built 65ft *Harvest Hope*. Around that time Dick, his father and his brother Ned chopped and changed from one boat to another, with both Dick and Ned also spending time on John Doyle's *Coreopsis*. The *Harvest Hope* was sold to a Gibraltar buyer in 1962. By then Dick had taken over from his father as skipper of the *Golden Quest* and did quite well with her up to the spring of 1965. Then he decided to look around for a bigger boat. Fishing a bigger boat required 'a ticket' – a fishing competency certificate. In order to gain that qualification he took time out and attended the appropriate course at Galway Technical College. While he was there a reconditioned BIM 50-footer came up for reissue. She was undergoing a makeover at Baltimore BIM Boatyard. Believing that he might have a chance of getting her, he forwarded an application to BIM Head Office. The 'powers that be' dillied and dallied for some time before reaching a positive decision! The cost of the boat was to be £6,500, so Dick placed a deposit based on that figure. Alas, when the actual issuing of the boat came around, as seems to have been the case in other BIM deals of that era, the cost had found its way upwards, on this occasion to £7,500. An agreement was reached by the parties concerned to split the difference, and on 13th September 1965 Dick took delivery of the *Ros Liath*, now fitted with a 120hp Kelvin engine, and indeed a new boat for all intents and purposes.

He went on to say, "Initially I fished the *Ros Liath* out of Howth and did really well trawling there. Around the end of October I came home to Dunmore East and headed for Helvick a place where I knew the fishing grounds well. There was plenty of fish there. Coming up to Christmas I recall buying one mid-water three bridle net, and two Engel bottom trawls. Poor catches from the mid-water net resulted in it being replaced by one of the bottom trawls. The effectiveness of that net has remained in my mind. On St Stephen's Night 1965 we left Waterford where we had been sheltering from bad weather and steamed straight for Baginbun. Each day of the week that followed we filled the boat with herring. The fish sold at £4.10/- a cran. In that week alone I recovered 1/3 of my outlay. That particular herring season lasted until the end of March. The Engel net had done a magnificent job!"

With the herring season over it was a case of back to trawling off Helvick. The routine was, "Leave Dunmore East on Sunday night, head for Helvick and fish until Tuesday evening. By then the boat was loaded down with fish, as much as I could put into her; sole, plaice and all that kind of fish. Because of the lack of transport from Dunmore East to the Dublin market we were obliged to steam to Duncannon, where we landed our fish for collection by the Kilmore Quay fish lorry on its way to Dublin. Having done so, we returned to Dunmore East, took stores on board and left for the fishing grounds off Helvick. The cycle began all over again. That went on for a number of years." Meanwhile, during the herring seasons, I mid-watered with a Duncannon boat, the BIM 50-footer *Maria*, owned and fished by Patsy Downes. Using small mid-water trawls purchased from Ivor Christiansen, Howth, (I.C. Trawls) we fished very successfully. Herring were so plentiful that we lost more than we boarded. When the herring went to the bottom at Baginbun, as other boats did, we changed to a bottom trawl."

In 1968 Dick decided the time had come to move up to an even bigger boat. He put the *Ros Liath* up for sale, and fished for awhile on John Doyle's *Xmas Morn*, a Scotch boat built at Fraserburgh in 1953. Later that year he purchased the 65ft *Coreopsis* from Gerry McLaughlin, Howth. Previously, the *Coreopsis* had been mechanically damage as result of taking a mooring rope on the propeller when fishing off the Kish. The outcome of that incident was a major overhaul carried out at Malahide Boatyard. It included the fitting of a fully reconditioned engine, a reconditioned gearbox, together with a new stern tube and shaft; all important factors in Dick's decision to purchase her. Initially he fished her out of Howth before returning to his old stamping ground at Helvick. Herring were still being caught by the boatload at Baginbun. During a couple of seasons bottom trawling there it became evident that the *Coreopsis* was underpowered. The 114hp Gardner wasn't enough! It was time to look around for a boat with a more powerful engine. His search led him to Scotland, where in 1972 he purchased the 152hp, 66ft *Sealgair*. "Having done", he said, "Well enough in her," mainly bottom trawling, he sold her within two years. While keeping an eye out for a suitable replacement he fished for a time on the *Golden Feather*, a Dunmore East boat owned by John Roche. On the grapevine he heard that Mick Orpen's 70ft, *Ardent*, a seiner built by Jones, Buckie was up for sale. Dick journeyed to Castletownbere where he met up with Mick and a deal was struck. In October 1974 the *Ardent*, re-named *Stelimar*, joined the Dunmore East fleet. Dick described her as, "A lovely boat, you couldn't get nicer." That winter he said, "I did very well herring pairing with the Castletownbere boat, *Patricia*, skippered and owned by Denis O'Driscoll."The following year saw the *Stelimar* herring pairing out of Howth with the Clogherhead boat *Fragrant Cloud*, owned and fished by Anthony Kirwan. Dick explained why that particular venture wasn't very successful, "The boats were underpowered. While the *Ardent* and *Fragrant Cloud* respectively had a 230hp and 240hp engines fitted, they really needed to be 400 or 500hp."

A Step Up

Following that one season fishing with the *Fragrant Cloud* he went back to trawling. That was in 1976. Dick recalled, "I was still in Howth and decided to try out a small black three bridled Swedish net that came with the *Stelimar* (*Ardent*) from Mick. The result was unbelievable! I caught loads of fish with it all through 1976 and '77! Mick of course kept an eye on how things were going and at one point in his own very special way, remarked, "You didn't buy the boat from me, I gave her to you."

As the years rolled on, good and all as the *Stelimar* was, her effectiveness in big time fishing came to an end. Steel hulled boats fitted with high powered engines, power blocks, net drums etc. became the order of the day. It was decision time for Dick. Should he treat himself for the first time in his career to a newly built boat or once again look towards a second-hand vessel. He decided on the former. Needing three quotations he approached boatyards at Arklow, Killybegs and Cobh. Maritime (Cobh) won the day. An order was placed in October 1979 for what was to be the new *Stelimar* (W146). The 19.02m x 17.98m x 6.16m x 2.79m vessel, powered by a 415hp/310kW main engine was to be ready for delivery in approximately 10 months. Maybe it was because the *Stelimar* was the first steel boat built at the yard, but for whatever reason delivery was in fact 10 months late.

Dick, Margaret (Peggy) and family on the occasion of the Stelimar launch. Courtesy D. Power.

When the order was placed for the building of *Stelimar* the Celtic Sea Herring Fishery had already been closed down. A year previously Dick replied to a Department of the Marine advertisement requesting applications from boat owners to carry out a herring larvae survey off the south coast. His application was successful and survey went on during the winters up to 1985, with the exception of 1980/'81 when it had to be suspended due to the fact that he had sold the original *Stelimar* and delivery of the new boat had fallen 10 months behind schedule. He didn't have a boat!

With the survey years behind them, and the Celtic Sea Herring Fishery again opened, Dick, his crew and the new *Stelimar* went back to mid-watering and prawn fishing. As result of one particular eight day fishing trip to the Smalls, prawns landed realised £16,000. A lot of money in those days! The *Stelimar*, under Dick's ownership, was to fish very successfully until he sold her to John Paul Healy, Durrus, Co Cork in 2004. However, in 1991 a major and tragic incident involving the *Stelimar* brought sadness and disbelief to Dunmore East and indeed to the fishing community nationwide. It's an incident that I'll refer to later.

***The Stelimar*. Courtesy D. Power.**

During the years Dick had the *Stelimar* he also owner two other boats. The first of those was the French built *Jonara* (W163), a 53ft timber hulled boat, fitted with a 415hp/309kW engine. She arrived at Dunmore East in February 1986. Re-winched, she pair-fished for a couple of years with the *Stelimar*, then skippered by Dunmore East man Denis Harding. Dick said, "Both did extremely well at prawns, whitefish and herring."

A Step Up

In 1988 Dick bought a third fishing boat, the *Exodus* (W577), a French built 53ft, timber hulled vessel, fitted with a 240hp/179kW engine. While she appeared to be in poor condition, examination of frames and planking showed her to be perfectly sound. The worst part, he said, "Was visible to the eye and above deck level. I bought her for £23,000 and with the help of a few shipwrights spent two months renovating her. I didn't keep her very long; maybe a year or a year-and-a-half, then I sold her on for £110,000."

As a matter of interest the name *Stelimar* was derived from the first three letters of Stephanie, the first two letter of Liam and the first three letters of Margaret, respectively the names of Dick's then children, and his wife.

That the children who came later didn't feel left out, the name *Jonara* was derived in similar fashion from John and Tara.

The years kept rolling on, Dick's family were growing up and in 1990 his eldest son Liam showed a keen interest in fishing. That being the case Dick advised the young man to study for 'a full ticket' at the National Fisheries College, Greencastle. That he did! Whether prompted by Liam's interest in fishing or not, Dick went ahead and bought a boat that came up for sale. She was the Malahide built, 68ft transom stern, *Star of Nazareth* (D38), a boat previously owned by Martin McLaughlin, Howth. Under the impression that a licence to fish for herring and mackerel would be granted Dick had the boat re-furbished, had a new engined fitted, and had a major winch overhaul carried out. She was ready to go fishing in the spring of 1991. The idea was that she would pair fish with the *Stelimar*. The licence did not materialise! Skippered initially by Dick, and later by the skipper of the then sold *Jonara*, and with Liam on the crew, the *Star of Nazareth* began to fish prawns at the Smalls. Efforts to procure a herring and mackerel fishing licence continued. To the man on the street it seemed incomprehensible and indeed grossly unfair that a licence was not granted given the circumstances, but rules are rules, and bureaucrats are bureaucrats. The circumstances were that pervious to the purchase of the *Star of Nazareth*, Dick owned three fishing boats, the *Stelimar*, the *Exodus* and the *Jonara*. He sold *Exodus* and the *Jonara* around the time he acquired the *Star of Nazareth*, surrendering the licences to fish herring and mackerel on each of the boats. That was on the assumption that he would be granted a corresponding licence for the *Star of Nazareth*. However, the bureaucrats reasoned otherwise – basically the surrendered licences on the two sold boats (*Exodus* and *Jonara*) were for all intent purposes dead as far as the application for a pelagic licence for the *Star of Nazareth* was concerned. One thing had nothing to do with the other! The focus was entirely on the entitlement of the boat to fish and an active history of fishing for herring and mackerel. While she had entitlement to fish for herring and mackerel she had no history of fishing for either of these species. Previous to purchase she was an existing boat within the fleet and, as the boat was over 65ft in length, the issue of a new licence was necessary. The purpose of that policy was to restrict fleet growth in the catching capacity of the pelagic sector where there was already over capacity.

The reality was that the *Star of Nazareth* was not to be granted a licence to catch herring and mackerel. So what was Dick to do, she wasn't much use to him without a licence. A change in circumstances due to the already mentioned tragic incident involving the *Stelimar* was later to affect the short time future of the *Star of Nazareth.* The sad tale as told by Dick unfolded as follows, "It was in 1991 and I had just returned from holiday. The *Stelimar* and the *Star of Nazareth* were fishing out of Howth. They both left on a particular Monday night to fish off the Kish. On the way a fire broke out in the *Stelimar*. I received a phone call at around 7.30am from the Dun Laoghaire Lifeboat Secretary informing me of the incident. The lifeboat and a cross channel ferryboat had assisted at the scene. The *Stelimar* had been very badly damaged by fire but worst of all a crew member, Jimmy Byrne, had tragically lost his life through smoke inhalation. The boat had been towed to Dun Laoghaire. I drove up to find a wreck of a boat and a crew plunged into disbelief at what had happened, and most of all by the loss of a colleague. I too, was shattered with disbelief. My abiding memory of the catastrophe is that of the outpouring of sympathy directed towards all concerned. It came from far and near and was a great comfort to the family of our deceased crewman and indeed to all of us."

So what was Dick to do with the *Stelimar*? Obviously she required a major makeover. To that end he had her towed to Howth where she underwent a total survey. That done her next destination was the Arklow Marine Services Boatyard. She was to stay at Arklow a long, long time and refurbishment costs were massive! With the work nearing completion attempts were made to start the engine. It proved a fruitless exercise! What had escaped the notice of all concerned was that on the fateful night water was hosed down through the *Stelimar's* funnel and into the engine by the crew of the cross channel ferryboat as they endeavoured to quench the fire. A further eight weeks had passed by the time the engine had been stripped down and rebuilt.

As mentioned earlier on, the *Stelimar* incident had a bearing on the short term future of the *Star of Nazareth.* It came about because of a magnanimous gesture by Department of the Marine bureaucrats! They allowed the *Stelimar's* mackerel and herring licence to be transferred to the *Star of Nazareth* for the duration of the *Stelimar's* layup. That made way for the *Star of Nazareth* to pair fish for herring with another boat. That winter she did so with the *Azure Sea* (D585), a boat then owned by Doran's of Howth.

The short term fix was still far from satisfactory. When the *Stelimar* returned to fishing the licence reverted back to her leaving the *Star of Nazareth* of little use to Dick. He had no option but to put her up for sale. Cecil Sharkey, Clogherhead, bought her. As a result Liam, now with his full ticket, had not got a boat to fish. Dick said, "He came fishing with me for awhile on the *Stelimar* and in time began fishing her himself, except for the herring seasons, when I came back. He did very well with her and we decided to have her re-engined, the winch refurbished and new shelter deck fitted. That work was done at Arklow in 1997. Liam continued to fish her in the years that immediately followed, but fishing as a career was beginning to go downhill a bit. Slowly but surely, for a variety of reasons, it emerged that Liam was unlikely to make fishing a lifetime career. I wasn't prepared to go back fulltime fishing myself. Factors such as unsociable working hours, difficulties with crews, the value of a normal family way of life, shore work for all concerned had become more attractive than fishing, and of course the fact that I wasn't getting any younger, all conspired to make up my mind to sell the *Stelimar*. In 2004 she became the property of John Paul Healy, and has been based at Union Hall ever since."

As referred to in the opening lines of this article Dick did not entirely retire from sea going. Almost immediately he decided to get a small boat, a boat that he could fish and manage himself. His quest led him to Kinsale where Fitzgerald Marine Manufacturing Ltd specialised in the production of a large range of fibreglass vessels. He explained his requirements to specialists at the Yard. In time a suitable mould was formed and the first steps of a process by which the boat would eventually emerge were set in motion. The *Dove* motored away from Kinsale in 2005. Dick has happily and leisurely fished her out of Dunmore East up to the present time.

In terms of shore activities related to fishing, Dick recalled that his father had been a founding member of the South & East Fishermen's Co-Operative Society, and that he himself had also been a member. Another local body in which Dick became active was the Dunmore East Fishermen's Co-Operative Society. In 1972 he became a committee member and was elected Chairman in 2002. Later he held the office of Executive Chairman from 2006 until his retirement in 2009. One year later, fishermen at the port were shocked and dismayed when informed by the Sea Fisheries Protection Authority that the handling, storage and sale of fish must cease immediately due to (you guessed it) EU regulations. The auction hall and cold storage facilities at the harbour's white fish landing berth, where over the years hundreds of thousand boxes of fish had been handled and auctioned, were wiped out by the stroke of yet another bureaucratic pen. It was a terrible blow to a village whose population was in decline, and to a port already struggling to overcome a range of problems.

The hazards associated with catching mercurial creatures of the sea are all too well known. Loss of life can result from so many causes! Fishing is unquestionably a dangerous way of making a living! Yet, no skipper or crew member believes disaster will befall them personally. For one reason or another misadventure becomes a reality!

The *Dove*- named after a boat owned by Dick's father many, many years ago! Credit P. Nolan.

So it was on the night of 22 September 1992! The Dunmore East 56ft, timber hulled fishing boat, *Orchidee,* was operating in darkness 50 miles off the south-east coast when she was run down by the large French fishing vessel *Agena*. The *Orchidee* sank quickly! Of the three crewmembers, two were missing; the third was recovered by the French vessel. As the accident happened in British territorial waters RAF helicopters were quickly on the scene. A Sikorsky helicopter from Shannon was also on its way within fifteen minutes. The search continued through the night and following day but the two missing men were not found. The incident could scarcely be closer to home for Dick, as one of the men who lost his life, the skipper and owner of the *Orchidee*, was his 28 year old brother Jimmy. The second casualty was little more than a youth, a

19 year old, named Bobby Doran of Bridgetown, Co Wexford. The lone survivor was Ken Pierce, then a 23 year old, and also from Bridgetown. What a reminder to all concerned of just how dangerous fishing at sea can be!

With the tape recorder safely put away, while we drank a cup of tea I sat on for awhile chatting with Dick and Margaret (Peggy). A topic which came up was Dick's involvement in what has been described as, 'incidents in the herring grounds off the south Wexford coast on 3 January 1966 between the crews of Northern Irish and Southern Irish trawlers'. The 'incidents' resulted in the following personnel being brought before the court, Michael Orpen, (*Ardent*) Bere Island, Co Cork; Mark Bates, (*Boolavogue*), Kilmore Quay, Co Wexford; William McCarthy (*Orien*) Sherkin Island, Co Cork; Michael Doran (*Silver Harvest*) Howth, Co Dublin and Richard (Dick) Power (*Rosliadha),* Newtown, Tramore, Co Waterford. All five were charged with unlawfully and maliciously damaging the Northern trawler, *Victory*, with intent to render it useless. The details of this case are long and arduous, but the pertinent point where Dick is concerned was that the spelling of his boat's name, correctly *Ros Liath*, proved too much for the authorities – there was no such boat as the *Rosliadha* involved in the incident – Dick had no case to answer! By the way all involved were found not guilty, though Mick Orpen had to go by a circuitous route to prove his innocence.

Following on, conversation drifted to the South & East Co-Op manager, Michael McSweeney, who lived across the road. I knew Michael (Mick) very well when we grew up together in Baltimore many years ago. I decided to drop in and see how he was doing. I was met at the door by a delightful young lady who introduced herself as Mick's daughter. Mick maintained that he recognised me from all those years ago but I can't help wondering if he had previous knowledge of my being in the Dunmore East area around that particular time. On the other hand, while Mick has naturally aged a little, I would still have known him had I met him on the street. He remembered that we played on the same football team but that the only photo of the team in existence shows him wearing an ordinary shirt of some kind, rather than a team jersey. Obviously times were tough and jerseys were in short supply! It was good meeting up with him again and the two personality plus ladies present, who were his married visiting daughters, kept the craic going.

There was just one more thing I planned to do before heading back to Waterford. That was to say hello to Sean and Kathleen O'Driscoll who lived in the Killea area. It was more or less on my way and I had been at the house a few months earlier when Sean recalled his fishing experiences for me. I drove along this narrow road and eventually arrived at a house which was that of Sean and Kathleen's - except that it wasn't. I knocked at the door but there was nobody home! Ah well, I'll put a wee note through the letter box! Sometime later an e-mail arrived from Kathleen suggesting that the next time I called it would be best if I came to her house rather than putting a note through her neighbour's letter box. There you are! A case of mistaken identity! One just can't win them all – it's true you know.

	No.	Name	Original Reg.	Year of Issue	First Homeport	Original Owner
Killybegs Built	1	*Ard Macha*	D207	1956	Teelin	Joe McGinley
	2	*St Catherine*	D299	1957	Killybegs	Seamus Murrin
	3	*Girl Eileen*	D13	1957	Killybegs	Mossie Moore
	4	*Ard Chluain*	D349	1958	Dingle	Louis Graham
	5	*Twilight Star*	D412	1958	Killybegs	Brian Gallagher
	6	*Roving Star*	D64	1959	Dingle	Patrick Sheehy
	7	*Coolan*	D90	1960	Dingle	P.Griffin & T. Sheehy
	8	*St Joseph*	D111	1960	Schull	Paddy O'Regan
	9	*Ard Chroine*	D237	1960	Burtonport	Joe Boyle
	10	*Ard Carna*	D328	1961	Killybegs	Thomas Murrin
	11	*Ard Finnian*	D402	1962	Howth	Paddy Sugrue
	12	*Morning Star*	D28	1964	Dingle	Joe Walsh
	13	*Ard Scia*	D55	1966	Kilronan	Kieran Gill
	14	*Ard Gillen*	D453	1967	Skerries	Tom Ferguson
	15	*Ard Aluinn*	D498	1968	Kilronan	Des Faherty
	16	*Connacht Ranger*	G47	1970	Kilronan	Gregory Conneely
Mevagh Built	1	*Ard Rathain*	D262	1956	Kilronan	Paraic McDonagh
	2	*San Marten*	D305	1957	Killybegs	George McCallig
	3	*Saoirse*	D346	1957	Raheen	Pat Deasy
	4	*St Bernadette*	D57	1958	Castletownbere	Gerry O'Shea
	5	*Ard Mhuire*	D5	1958	Burtonport	Willie Joe McBride
	6	*Ard Colm*	D37	1959	Non-permanent	BIM Training
	7	*Ard Ailbhe*	D198	1960	Dun Laoghaire	Brian Crummy
	8	*Ard Fionnbarr*	D370	1961	Dingle	Michael Flannery

	9	*Ard Aidhm*	D378	1961	Dun Laoghaire	Ronan Mallon
	10	*Ard Ide*	D344	1962	Dingle	John Brosnan
	11	*Ard Aengus*	Unknown	1964	Kilronan	Gregory Conneely
Tyrrell Built	1	*Glendalough*	D310	1957	Arklow	Bill Cleary
	2	*Glenmalure*	D147	1957	Arklow	Jack Bermingham
	3	*Naomh Brendain*	D79	1959	Dingle	Joe Flaherty
	4	*Sancta Lucia*	D4	1959	Cahirciveen	Jimmy O'Sullivan
	5	*Ard Dallan*	D240	1960	Burtonport	Joe McBride
	6	*Ard Ciaran*	D311	1960	Clogherhead	Oliver Tallon
Baltimore Built	1	*Ard Eireann*	D106	1964	Dingle	Paudie Curran
	2	*Ard Beara*	D462	1967	Castletownbere	Paddy Harrington
Crosshaven Built	1	*Ard Casta*	D321	1957	Cape Clear Isl.	Ernie O'Driscoll
	2	*Ard Mor*	D277	1957	Helvick	Batt Whelan
Dingle Built	1	*Guiding Star*	D2	1964	Dingle	Paddy Flaherty
	2	*Favourite*	SO351	1971	Burtonport	James Gallagher

Clachan's 'Historic Irish Journeys' series

Travels In Ireland - J.G. Kohl

This is a very readable account by a German visitor of his tour around Ireland immediately before the Great Famine.

Disturbed Ireland – 1881 - Bernard Becker

A series of letters written as the author travelled around the West of Ireland, visiting key places in the 'Land War'. We meet Captain Boycott and other members of the gentry, as well as a range of small farmers and peasants.

A Journey throughout Ireland, During the Spring, Summer and Autumn of 1834 - Henry D. Inglis

Inglis travels Ireland attempting to answer the question, 'is Ireland and improving country?' using discussion with landlords, manufacturers and tenants plus his own insightful observations.

The West Of Ireland: Its Existing Condition and Prospects - Henry Coulter

This is a collection of letters from *Saunders's News-Letter* relating to the condition and prospects of the people of the West of Ireland after the partial failure of the harvests of the early 1860s.

Highways and Byways in Donegal and Antrim - Stephen Gwynn

Take this book with you as you travel around Donegal and the Glens of Antrim and you will find that you journey not only over land, but also over time.

* * * * *

Clachan 'Local History' Series

Henry Coulter's account has been sub-divided for the convenience of local and family historians.

The West Of Ireland: Its Existing Condition and Prospects, Part 1, by Henry Coulter. This is an extract from the complete edition dealing with Athlone, Co. Clare and Co. Galway.

The West Of Ireland: Its Existing Condition and Prospects, Part 2, by Henry Coulter. This is an extract from the complete edition dealing with Co. Mayo.

The West Of Ireland: Its Existing Condition and Prospects, Part 3, by Henry Coulter. The final extract from the complete edition dealing with Counties Co Sligo, Donegal, Leitrim and Roscommon.

* * * * *

J.G.Kohl's account has been sub-divided for the convenience of local and family historians.

Travels in Ireland – Part 1, takes us through Edgeworthtown, The Shannon, Limerick, Edenvale, Kilrush and Father Mathew.

Travels in Ireland – Part 2, his journey continues through Tarbet, Tralee, Killarney, Bantry, Cork, Kilkenny and Waterford.

Travels in Ireland – Part 3, this section deals with Wexford, Enniscorthy, Avoca, Glendalough and Dublin.

Travels In Ireland - Part 4 – he goes north for the last part of his journey through Dundalk, Newry, Belfast, The Antrim Coast, Rathlin, The Giant's Causeway.

* * * * *

Henry D. Inglis' account has also been sub-divided for the convenience of local and family historians.

A Journey throughout Ireland, During the Spring, Summer and Autumn of 1834, Part 1 takes us from Dublin. Through Wexford, Waterford and Cork.

A Journey throughout Ireland, During the Spring, Summer and Autumn of 1834, Part 2 is an account of Kerry, Clare, Limerick and the Shannon and concludes in Athlone.

* * * * *

Stephen Gwynn's account has also been sub-divided for the convenience of local and family historians.

Highways and Byways in Donegal and Antrim Part One: Donegal

Highways and Byways in Donegal and Antrim Part: Two - Derry & Co. Antrim

* * * * *

Aghaidh Achadh Mór, The Face of Aghamore – edited by Joe Byrne. This is a reproduction of a title originally published in 1991 and is of enduring interest to local historians and to those with ancestral roots in East Mayo. It covers such topics as Stone Age archaeology, family history, local hedge schools, O'Carolan's connection with the parish, the Civil War and townland surveys.

Lough Corrib, Its Shores and Islands: with Notices of Lough Mask - by William R. Wilde, first published in 1867. In the words of the author: 'A work intended to … rescue from oblivion, or preserve from desecration, some of the historic monuments of the country'.

A Statistical and Agricultural Survey of the Co. of Galway – by Hely Dutton

Dutton's survey has resulted in a detailed description of the agricultural conditions and practices of Galway in the early Nineteenth Century. He has added detailed chronologies of the leading officials of Galway town and its governance, as well as of the senior churchmen of the bishopric of Tuam and the abbeys, monasteries and convents, of the area.

A History of Sligo: Town and Country, Vol. I, by Terrence O'Rorke

This classic and well-loved history, first published in 1889, is the work of a man born and bred in Sligo. It remains a work of fascination for anyone with connections to Sligo, and is an important reference for anyone interested in the history of Ireland.

* * * * *

Poems, Ballads and Songs

Songs of the Glens of Antrim, Moiré O'Neill

These Songs of the Glens of Antrim were written by a Glenswoman in the dialect of the Glens, and chiefly for the pleasure of other Glens-people.

Away with Words – by Michael Sands

This Newry born traditional musician and poet has marred into North Antrim where he is raising a family. His poems are bedded in these ordinary realities which he observes with a fresh and quiet sensitivity, infused with affection and love.

Clachan Publishing, Ballycastle, Glens of Antrim.

www.ingramcontent.com/pod-product-compliance
Ingram Content Group UK Ltd.
Pitfield, Milton Keynes, MK11 3LW, UK
UKHW012225240726
13966UKWH00003B/951